Back to Basics

The Alcoholics Anonymous
Beginners' Meetings

Back to Basics

The Alcoholics Anonymous Beginners' Meetings

"Here are the steps we took . . . "
in Four One-Hour
Sessions

Wally P.

Faith With Works Publishing Company
Tucson, AZ

Published by Faith With Works Publishing Company
P.O. Box 91648, Tucson, AZ 85752-1648
tel: (520) 297-9348 / fax: (520) 297-7230 / e-mail: wallyp@theriver.com
http://www.aabacktobasics.org

First Edition: 1997
Second Edition, New and Revised: 1998
    First–Fourth Printings: 1998-2000
Second Edition, New Size and Revised: 2001
    Fifth–Eight Printings: 2001-2014
    Ninth Printing: January 2015

Library of Congress Cataloging -in-Publication Data

P., Wally, 1945-
Back to basics: the alcoholics anonymous beginners' meetings
        p.   cm.
    Includes bibliographical references and appendices
    LCCN: 2001-131462
    ISBN 13: 978-0-9657720-1-3
    ISBN 10: 0-9657720-1-2

1. Alcoholics Anonymous. 2. Alcoholism-Recovery. 3. Addiction-Recovery. 4. Obsessive/Compulsive Behavior Recovery. 5. Twelve-step Program. I. Title

We gratefully acknowledge permission granted by Alcoholics Anonymous World Services, Inc. to quote from Conference Approved publications with source attributions. The publication of this volume does not imply affiliation with, nor approval or endorsement from, Alcoholics Anonymous World Services, Inc.

Printed in the United States of America

Dedication

This book is dedicated to Dr. Bob., cofounder of Alcoholics Anonymous. In the mid 1940's, he authorized the publication of a pamphlet titled *A Guide to the Twelve Steps of Alcoholics Anonymous,* which was based on "a series of instruction classes conducted by veteran members of A.A." in Akron, Ohio. Later, he endorsed *The Little Red Book,* which evolved from the "Twelve Step Study Classes" conducted by the Nicollet Group in Minneapolis, Minnesota.

This book is also dedicated to the numerous A.A. pioneers who led Beginners' Meetings during the early days of the fellowship. In the 1940's and 1950's, tens of thousands of men and women recovered from the affliction of alcoholism by taking the Twelve Steps in four one-hour sessions. In the process, they discovered a God of their understanding and a new way of living based on the guidelines of **"Trust in God . . . clean house"** and **"Help others."**

In addition, the author wishes to acknowledge the hundreds of thousands of A.A.'s who are currently involved in Beginners' Meetings throughout the world. You are keeping Dr. Bob's "keep it simple" legacy alive and, at the same time, proving that the Beginners' Meetings of today can be just as effective as those held more than sixty years ago.

Authors note: I do not believe in "making money out of A.A." Any proceeds from this book, after out-of-pocket expenses are met, will be used to distribute books at no cost to individuals and A.A. groups who cannot afford to buy them.

Contents

Acknowledgments

After two years of extensive research at A.A. archival repositories throughout the United States and Canada, more than one hundred interviews of old-timers who attended Beginners' Meetings in the 1940's, and one year of leading the four one-hour sessions, I thought this book was ready for publication. Then in December 1996, one of my "spiritual guides" gave me a call. He challenged me to take as much of "Wally P." out of **Back to Basics** as possible. He said, "The last thing this fellowship needs is another book expounding someone's personal opinions on how the Steps should be taken. Too many people have already 'muddied the water' by presenting their own interpretations of the original program." I took his message to heart, especially since he had been personally involved with Beginners' Meetings for more than forty years.

So, I set out to edit as much of "Wally P." out of these pages as possible. During the next six months, I conducted **Back to Basics** Seminars in Burbank, CA; Phoenix, AZ; East Dorset, VT; and Center City, MN. Based on feedback from attendees, I revised the format to improve continuity and clarity. I then released the first edition of the book in August 1997.

The response was overwhelmingly positive. By word of mouth, news of **Back to Basics** spread across the United States and then around the world. Many A.A.'s started their own **Back to Basics** Beginners' Meetings and Groups. Reports of recoveries came in by the thousands.

ix

Based on subsequent *Back to Basics* seminars, additional information from old-timers, and a letter from the A.A. General Services Office suggesting that we remove the words "classes" and "instructors" from the text, I revised the book in 1998. Since then, I have made only minor changes to this "original" A.A. meeting format.

In the eighteen years (1997-2015) since the book's publication, more than five hundred thousand people have **TAKEN** the Twelve Steps in *Back to Basics* meetings and seminars. Many who had been in and out of A.A. for years, report a **"new way of living"** as the direct result of **TAKING** the Steps in four one-hour sessions. This very effective and highly successful **"program of action"** played an important role in A.A.'s early history and is playing an equally important role today.

I wish to thank those who provided archival material and their firsthand experiences for this book. In keeping with the spirit of **"principles before personalities,"** I have recorded only the cities in which they reside:

Akron, OH	Boston, MA	Center City, MN
Chula Vista, CA	Cleveland, OH	Dallas, TX
Denver, CO	Detroit, MI	E. Wallingford, VT
Eddyville, OR	Gary, IN	Harsen Island, MI
Independence, OH	Jacksonville, FL	Joplin, MO
Little Rock, AR	Long Beach, CA	Los Angeles, CA
Maysville, AR	Miami, FL	Minneapolis, MN
Newton Falls, OH	N. Hollywood, CA	Oklahoma City, OK
Palmer, TX	Palmdale, CA	Palm Springs, CA
Philadelphia, PA	Phoenix, AZ	Pompano Beach, FL
Prescott, AZ	Rogersville, MO	Seattle, WA
Sebastian, FL	Seminole, FL	Sonora, CA
Spring, TX	Sun City, AZ	Sun City West, AZ
Timonium, MD	Vancouver, B.C.	Venice, CA
Washington, D.C.	Washingtonville, NY	Windsor, Ontario

Back to Basics

The Alcoholics Anonymous
Beginners' Meetings

Introduction

Prior to the publication of this book in 1997, the Beginners' Meetings were a forgotten piece of Alcoholics Anonymous history. Very few people in recovery knew anything about the four one-hour sessions that played such an important role in the initial success of the Twelve Step movement.

These meetings were held throughout the United States and Canada during a period of time when A.A. enjoyed a 50 to 75 percent recovery rate from alcoholism. Newcomers quickly learned **"How it Works."** They had conversion experiences, discovered a new way of living without alcohol, and carried their message of hope to others.

By taking the Twelve Steps in these Beginners' Meetings, tens of thousands of A.A.'s found the spiritual solution to alcoholism. They completed the Steps in about a month. Then in order to ensure their own sobriety, they helped others through the recovery process.

This book is a re-enactment of the sessions as they were held in the mid 1940's. This A.A. meeting format is based solely on the author's interpretation of the available source material.

In the early days, no two meeting leaders conducted these sessions in exactly the same way. This is also true today. We urge those interested in starting an A.A. Beginners' Meeting to use this format as a guide — a starting point. Feel free to modify this program, but please keep in mind that those who have remained true to Dr. Bob's "keep it simple" philosophy have had the greatest success.

In the 1940's, there was little controversy surrounding the Beginners Meetings. They served a very important purpose–to save lives. Even Bill W, one of the cofounders of A.A., insisted that we let God rather than "control committees" guide us in our life-saving efforts. In September 1945, he wrote an article for *The Grapevine* in which he stated that if A.A. were to succeed, it must be governed by God rather than by rules or rule makers:

> "Were we to proceed by rules, somebody would have to make them and, more difficult still, somebody would have to enforce them. 'Rule-making' has often been tried. It usually results in controversy among the 'rule makers' as to what the rules should be. . . .
>
> "Our experience tells us these universal truths (the 12 Steps) work. (We are) ruled, not by people, but by principles . . . and, as most of us would say, (we are) ruled by God."

This concept later became the cornerstone of A.A.'s Second Tradition, which states, "For our group purpose there is but *one ultimate authority*, a loving God as He may express Himself in our group conscience." Throughout the United States and Canada during the 1940's and 1950's, many A.A. Groups were guided to start Beginners' Meetings. These meetings provided newcomers with a safe and structured environment in which to take the Twelve Steps and recover from alcoholism.

Chapter One contains a small portion of the written record

on the Beginners' Meetings. This information confirms that these sessions were an integral part of the early success of Alcoholics Anonymous.

Chapters Two through Five are re-enactments of the four one-hour Beginners' Meetings as conducted in 1946. In these sessions, the author has tried to remain true to the "Big Book" as well as to the old-timers who originally led these meetings.

Chapter Six provides additional insight into the inner workings of the Beginners' Meetings. In the 1940's, A.A.'s used an assets and liabilities checklist to take the Fourth and Fifth Steps. During daily "quiet times," they conducted a written Eleventh Step. By remaining involved for three to six months, they learned how to sponsor others through these four one-hour sessions.

In the mid-1940's there was only one Twelve Step program and only one book that described the spiritual solution to alcoholism–the "Big Book" of *Alcoholics Anonymous*. Since then, the book has been a great help for those with other difficulties. But, because Back to Basics is an A.A. meeting format, we ask that:

> "If you have a problem other than alcohol, substitute your addiction, affliction or compulsive behavior for the word alcohol each time you see or hear it during these Beginners' Meetings. If you do this, you, too, will recover as the direct result of taking **ALL** Twelve Steps in four one-hour sessions."

Although a considerable amount of recovery literature has been written since the "Big Book," it is still the only publication that provides the directions on how to take the Steps. *Alcoholics Anonymous* contains clear and concise instructions on how to develop an intimate, two-way relationship with the **"Power greater than ourselves,"** that resides **"deep down within us."**

The "Big Book" authors tell us that this Power will **"accomplish those things for us which we could never do by ourselves.** By taking the Steps, we identify and remove the blocks that have separated us from this Power so we can listen to and follow the **"God-consciousness within."** The authors provide us with a simple test to separate self-will from God's will. They emphasize that **"working with others"** is essential in order to **"keep in fit spiritual condition."**

On page 59, the "Big Book" authors describe the solution to all of our problems:

> **". . . there is One who has all power—that One is God. May you find Him now!"**

Chapter 1

Evolution of the A.A. Beginners' Meetings

When *Alcoholics Anonymous* was first published in April 1939, the "Big Book" authors claimed that one hundred had recovered from alcoholism since June 1935. This slow rate of growth was partially due to the lack of written instructions on the **"course of action":**

5 recovered at the end of 1935
15 recovered at the end of 1936
40 recovered at the end of 1937
100 recovered at the end of 1938

Shortly after the publication of *Alcoholics Anonymous*, a fellowship evolved based on the principles of the book. The organization was so successful in providing a solution for the **"hopeless state of mind and body "** known as alcoholism that it received a considerable amount of public interest and support. This publicity resulted in increased book sales and membership:

400 recovered at the end of 1939
2,000 recovered at the end of 1940
8,000 recovered at the end of 1941

Much of the early growth took place in Cleveland, Ohio as the result of a series of newspaper articles published in the *Cleveland Plain Dealer*, starting on October 21, 1939. The fellowship gained national prominence with the release of an article on Alcoholics Anonymous, written by Jack Alexander in

5

the March 1, 1941 issue of the *Saturday Evening Post*. By 1950, membership had increased to 100,000. Since then, membership doubled every 10 years until the early 1990's.

With the rapid initial growth in Cleveland came the need for meetings in which new A.A. members could be quickly taken through the Twelve Steps:

> "It was soon evident that a scheme of personal sponsorship would have to be devised for the new people. Each prospect was assigned an older A.A., who visited him at his home, or in the hospital, instructed him on A.A. principles, and conducted him to his first meeting. But in the face of many hundreds of pleas for help, the supply of elders couldn't possibly match the demand. Brand-new A.A.'s, sober only a month or even a week, had to sponsor alcoholics still drying up in the hospitals." [1]

Because of the rapid influx of people looking for a solution to their drinking problem, newly sober members had to grasp the basic principles of the program in a very short period of time. They were then pressed into service helping others through the Twelve Steps. This method was very successful as evidenced by the early recovery rates in Cleveland:

> "Yes, Cleveland's results were the best. Their results were in fact so good, and A.A.'s membership else-

---

1 Anonymous, *Alcoholics Anonymous Comes of Age* (New York, NY: Alcoholics Anonymous Publishing, Inc., 1957, 1958) 20-21.

where was so small, that many a Clevelander really thought A.A. had started there in the first place." [2]

"Records in Cleveland showed that 93% of those who came to us never had a drink again." [3]

During the winter of 1941, the Crawford Group, which had been founded in February of that year, organized a separate meeting to help newcomers through the Steps. By the first issue of the Cleveland *Central Bulletin*, published in October 1942, the Crawford Beginners' Meetings were a well-established part of the Cleveland A.A. program:

Crawford Training–8920 Euclid Ave.–Sunday, 8:30 p.m. [4]

The November 1942 issue of the *Central Bulletin* contained an article titled "Crawford Men's Training," which described the structure and effectiveness of the Cleveland Beginners' Meetings. This article also provided the first written evidence that the Beginners' Meetings had spread to A.A. communities outside of Cleveland:

---

2 Anonymous, *Alcoholics Anonymous Comes of Age* (New York, NY: Alcoholics Anonymous Publishing, Inc., 1957, 1958) 21-22.

3 Anonymous, *Dr. Bob and the Good Oldtimers* (New York, NY: Alcoholics Anonymous World Services Inc., 1980) 261.

4 Anonymous, *Central Bulletin* (Cleveland, OH: Central Committee, October 1942) 2.

CRAWFORD MEN'S TRAINING

"The Crawford Men's Training System has been highly acclaimed to many. Older A.A.'s are asked to come to these meetings . . . where new prospects will be given individual attention just as though they were in a hospital. Visiting a prospect in his home has always been handicapped by interruptions, by the prospect not daring to unburden himself completely for fear of being overheard by his relatives, and by the A.A.'s reticence for the same reason. Hospitalization without question is the ideal answer to where the message will be most effective, but the Crawford Training Plan strikes us as being the next best.

"This group has even had regular visitors from Pittsburgh and surrounding small towns." [5]

The January 1943 issue of the Cleveland *Central Bulletin* contains a letter from the Washington, DC Group asking about the Crawford Group's Beginners' Meetings. This letter established a link between the Cleveland, Ohio Beginners' Meetings and Washington, DC. The Washington, DC Group started a Beginners' Meeting shortly afterward:

"I enjoyed your Bulletins very much. Would appreciate it if you would let me know what the 'Crawford Men's Training System' is and how it operates.

"We need a good plan for new members and pros-

---

5 Anonymous, *Central Bulletin* (Cleveland, OH: Central Committee, November 1942) 2.

pects here, . . . and this might be of great help to us." [6]

The Editor of the *Central Bulletin* responded with a letter describing the Crawford Group Beginners' Meetings. The sessions were "sponsored" by the Crawford Men's Group:

> "The Crawford Training Meeting is held in the Crawford Men's group club rooms at 8920 Euclid Ave. The members of this group have had several members who cannot be hospitalized, either because they are sober at the time, or cannot afford it. So as a substitute for hospitalization, a meeting is held on Sunday afternoons. Older members of the group attend, and talk to the prospects." [7]

The Beginners' Meetings continued at the Euclid Ave. meeting hall through June 1943. At that time the *Central Bulletin* announced the formation of a second session:

MILES TRAINING MEETINGS

> "The Miles Group reports they have enjoyed unusual success with their training meetings. The newcomer is not permitted to attend a regular meeting until he has been given a thorough knowledge of the work of A.A. From 15 to 20 participate at each training meeting and

---

6 Anonymous, *Central Bulletin* (Cleveland, OH: Central Committee, January 1943) 4.

7 Anonymous, *Central Bulletin* (Cleveland, OH: Central Committee, January 1943) 4.

new members are thoroughly 'indoctrinated.' These meetings are held at (the) _____ Floral Shop, 4141 E. 116th St." [8]

In January 1944, the Crawford Men's Group changed it's name to the Doan Men's Group and moved their Beginners' Meetings to 2028 E. 105th Street. The March 1944 *Central Bulletin* contained an update on the Doan Men's Group lifesaving activities:

> "The Sunday Training Sessions continue to be popular, attracting 30-40 members, who bring from 5 to 10 new men in each week." [9]

The Doan Men's Group Beginners' Meetings were mentioned again in the May 1944 *Central Bulletin*. By this time the sessions had become so successful that the Doan Men's Group members requested that all groups in Cleveland send their newcomers to their meetings:

> "The Sunday Training Meeting has been advanced to 3:00 pm, and we are repeating our invitation to all groups to bring their prospects to this meeting before they're actually ready to be enrolled in your group. The facilities are splendid for private interviews, as

---

8 Anonymous, *Central Bulletin* (Cleveland, OH: Central Committee, June 1943) 3.

9 Anonymous, *Central Bulletin* (Cleveland, OH: Central Committee, March 1944) 4.

well as to hear a leader explain the basic principles." [10]

This announcement confirmed that, as early as the spring of 1944, the Beginners' Meetings were already a prerequisite for joining an A.A. group in Cleveland. The Cleveland A.A.'s felt it was essential that newcomers be familiar with the "basic principles" before ever attending a "regular" meeting of Alcoholics Anonymous.

As A.A. grew and spread throughout the country, Beginners' Meetings became an integral part of the recovery process in many areas outside of Cleveland. In June 1943, the North-West Group of Detroit, Michigan, standardized the meetings into four sessions:

> "In June 1943, a group of members proposed the idea of a separate discussion meeting to more advantageously present the Twelve Steps of the Recovery Program to the new affiliates and a decision was made to hold a closed meeting for alcoholics only for this purpose. The first discussion meeting of the North-West Group was held at 10216 Plymouth Road on Monday night, June 14, 1943, and has been held every Monday night without exception thereafter [as of 1948]. A plan of presentation of the Twelve Steps of the Recovery Program was developed at this meeting. This plan consisted of dividing the Twelve Steps into Four

---

10 Anonymous, *Central Bulletin* (Cleveland, OH: Central Committee, May 1944) 3.

In many areas of the United States and Canada, the newcomer could not attend "regular" meetings of Alcoholics Anonymous until he or she had completed all Twelve Steps in the Beginners' Meetings. Wilfred W., of Windsor, Ontario, Canada, had his last drink on October 22, 1943. Six weeks later, he received his Sobriety Card which showed that he had completed the Steps on December 10, 1943. Wilfred then became one of the thousands of "card carrying" members of Alcoholics Anonymous.

categories for easier study and the divisions were: (1) Admission (2) Spiritual (3) Restitution and Inventory (4) Working and Message. Each division came to be discussed on each succeeding Monday night in rotation and this method was so successful that it was adopted, first by other groups in Detroit and then throughout the United States and finally was published in its entirety by the Washington, D.C. Groups in a pamphlet entitled: 'An Interpretation of the Twelve Steps'." [11]

Wilfred W., A.A. number three in Windsor, Ontario, Canada, recalled during a video taped interview on February 14, 1988 that the first A.A. meeting in that city was held on October 22, 1943. In addition to Wilfred and several other locals, there were three A.A.'s from Detroit in attendance.

Windsor, Ontario emulated the Detroit A.A. structure. The group held three meetings each week, an Open Meeting, a Closed Meeting and a Beginners' Meeting. The Beginners' Meeting consisted of four sessions in which the "babies" were taken through the Twelve Steps. The steps were divided into essentially the same classifications as Detroit. Wilfred described the classifications as "Admittance," "Spiritual," "Inventory" and "Carrying the Message." [12]

---

11 Two-page insert bound to the inside cover of a First Edition / Early Printing (4th or 5th) of the book *Alcoholics Anonymous.*

12 Video tape interview of Wilfred W., conducted by Dave W., on February 14, 1988.

By the end of 1943, the Jacksonville, Florida Group was sponsoring a Beginners' Meeting. Their weekly meeting schedule listed one General Meeting open to the public and six Group Meetings for members only. In addition, on Tuesday evenings at 8:30 pm, newcomers were taken through the Twelve Steps:

Tuesday ....Beginner's Class [13]

The Washington, DC Group pamphlet titled *Alcoholics Anonymous–An Interpretation of the Twelve Steps* was first published in September 1944. It contains twenty pages of specific instructions for leading Beginners' Meetings. The pamphlet was edited by "Uncle Dick" (Richard J.) and published by Paragon Press.

The pamphlet opens with this statement:

"These meetings are held for the purpose of acquainting both old and new members with the 12 Steps on which our program is based.

"So that all 12 Steps may be covered in a minimum of time, they are divided into four classifications. One evening each week will be devoted to each of the four subdivisions. Thus, in one month, a new man can get the basis of our 12 suggested Steps.

Discussion #1—The admission, Step 1.
Discussion #2—The spiritual phase, Steps 2, 3, 5, 6, 7,

---

13   Anonymous, *A.A. Jacksonville Group* (Jacksonville, FL: Jacksonville Group, 1943) 2

and 11.
Discussion #3—The inventory and restitution, Steps
4, 8, 9, and 10.
Discussion #4—The active work, Step 12." [14]

Intergroup and Central Offices throughout the United States
and Canada reproduced this pamphlet during the 1940's and
1950's. The A.A. of Greater Detroit Intergroup Office still dis-
tributes the pamphlet today.

In the fall of 1944, a copy of the Washington, D.C. pamphlet
reached Barry C., one of the A.A. pioneers in Minneapolis, Minnesota. He wrote a letter to the New York Headquarters request-
ing permission to distribute the pamphlet. Bobbie Berger, Secretary to Bill W. and the Alcoholic Foundation, sent this reply:

". . .The Washington pamphlet like the new Cleveland
one and the host of others are all local projects. . . . We
do not actually approve or disapprove of these local
pieces, by that I mean that the Foundation feels each
Group is entitled to write up its own 'can opener' (and)
let it stand on its own merits. All of them have good
points and very few have caused any (controversy).
But as in all things of a local nature, we keep hands off,
either pro or con. . . . Frankly, I (haven't) had time to
(more) than glance at the Washington booklet but I've
heard some favorable comments about it. I think there

14 Anonymous, *Alcoholics Anonymous–An Interpretation of Our Twelve Steps* (Washington, D.C.: Paragon
Creative Printers, September 1944) 1-2.

must be at least 25 local pamphlets now being used and I've yet to see one that hasn't some good points. I think it is up to each individual Group whether it wants to use and buy these pamphlets from the Group that puts them out." [15]

In 1945, *The Grapevine* printed three articles on the Beginners' Meetings. The first one, published in the June issue, described how the meetings were conducted in St. Louis, Missouri. This article contained the statement that newcomers could not become members of the local A.A. group until they had taken all Twelve Steps:

> "The Wilson Club, one of the four St. Louis A.A. groups, is now using a very satisfactory method of 'educating' prospects and new members. It has done much to reduce the number of slippers among new members. In brief, it is somewhat as follows: Each new prospect is asked to attend four successive Thursday night meetings, each one of which is devoted to helping the new man learn something about Alcoholics Anonymous, its founding, and the way it works. The new man is told something about the book, and how this particular group functions. . . .
>
> "Wilson Club members are not considered full, active members until they have attended these four edu-

---

15 Letter from Margaret R. Burger, New York, NY, on "The Alcoholic Foundation" letterhead to Barry C., Minneapolis, MN, dated November 11, 1944.

cational meetings." [16]

In the September 1945 issue of *The Grapevine*, the Genesee Group of Rochester, New York explained their format for taking newcomers through the Steps. Here we find yet one more reference to the fact that, in many areas of the United States, a newcomer had to complete all Twelve Steps before becoming a member of the local A.A. group:

> ". . . It has been our observation that bringing men into the group indiscriminately, and without adequate preliminary training and information, can be a source of considerable grief and a cause of great harm to the general morale of the group itself. We feel that unless a man, after a course of instruction and an intelligent presentation of the case for the A.A. life, has accepted it without any reservation, he should not be included in group membership. When his sponsors feel that the novice has a fair working knowledge of A.A.'s objectives and a sufficient grasp of its fundamentals, he is then brought to his first group meeting.

> ". . . There he listens to four successive talks based on the 12 Steps and the Four Absolutes. There are twenty-minute talks given by older members of the group and the steps, for convenience and brevity, are divided into four sections. The first three steps constitute the text of the first talk. The next four, the second; the next four, the third; and the last step is considered

---

16 Anonymous, *The Grapevine* (New York, NY: The Alcoholic Foundation, Vol. II, No. 1, June 1945) 4.

to be entitled to a full evening's discussion by itself." [17]

In the December 1945 issue of *The Grapevine*, the St. Paul, Minnesota Group wrote a full, one page description of their Beginners' Meetings. This group was large enough to conduct all four sessions simultaneously:

"The present plan of discussions for new members in the St. Paul Group . . . has been in operation for seven months . . . and [is] . . . based on the material presented in the Washington, D.C., pamphlet and obtained from other sources.

"Four discussions covering the A.A. program were outlined. Two members for each of these prepared and presented their discussions before the remainder of the group. Critical attention to these 'previews' enabled each individual to reorganize or rewrite his discussion so that it would contain what the group as a whole considered an adequate presentation of the subject on the basis of their collective experience and what they knew of experiences elsewhere.

"In general, the plan is to cover the A.A. program as clearly, concisely and completely as possible in four 45-minute discussions, with time for questions at the end of each. The arrangement of the clubrooms permits all four discussions to be presented at one time, each in a separate room, every Wednesday evening. New mem-

17 Anonymous, *The Grapevine* (New York, NY: The Alcoholic Foundation, Vol. II, No. 4, September 1945) 6.

bers are urged to attend all of the sessions in the proper order." [18]

In 1945, Barry C. of Minneapolis, Minnesota, received a letter from one of the members of the Peoria, Illinois Group. In the letter, Bud described the efforts of the Peoria Group to start a Beginners' Meeting. He wrote that it was the Peoria Group conscience to require all existing as well as prospective A.A. members to attend the four sessions:

"In my usual slow and cautious manner I have proceeded to sell the Peoria Group on the Nicollet Group. Tomorrow night we all meet to vote the adoption of your by-law, slightly altered to fit local conditions. Sunday afternoon at 4:30 our first class in the 12 Steps begins. We're all attending the first series of classes so we'll all be on an even footing. We anticipate losing quite a few fair-weather A.A. hangers-on in the elimination automatically imposed by the rule that these classes must be attended. This elimination we anticipate with a wee feeling of suppressed pleasure in-as-much as we are all extremely fed up with running a free drunk taxi and sobering up service." [19]

The July 1945 issue of *The Grapevine* contained an article that listed nineteen characteristics of a good sponsor. In the list

---

18 Anonymous, *The Grapevine* (New York, NY: The Alcoholic Foundation, Vol. II, No. 7, December 1945) 4.

19 Letter from Bud _., Peoria, IL, to Barry C., Minneapolis, MN, dated Friday 13, 1945.

were two direct references to the Beginners' Meetings:

> 4. Come to all the classes (Beginners' Meetings) with the new member.
>
> 5. If a new member alibis about coming to the classes (Beginners' Meetings), . . . the sponsor should impress upon him the importance of attendance at these meetings. [20]

Sometime prior to 1946, the Akron, Ohio Group started publishing a series of four pamphlets on the A.A. Program. Evan W. wrote them at the direction of Dr. Bob, one of the co-founders of Alcoholics Anonymous.

Dr. Bob wanted some "Blue Collar A.A. pamphlets" for the fellowship because he felt the "Big Book" was too complicated for many newcomers. He asked Evan to present "The Recovery Program" in its most basic terms.

The introduction to the pamphlet titled *Guide to the Twelve Steps* contains a reference to the Akron, Ohio Beginners' Meetings:

> "A GUIDE to the Twelve Steps of Alcoholics Anonymous is intended as a simple, short and concise interpretation of the rules for sober living as compiled by the earliest members of the organization. The writers and editors are members of the Akron, Ohio group—

---

20 Anonymous, *The Grapevine* (New York, NY: The Alcoholic Foundation, Vol. II, No. 2, July 1945) 4.

where Alcoholics Anonymous was founded in 1935.
. . . Most of the ideas and explanations were brought
out in a series of instruction classes conducted by veteran members of the group.

"The Twelve Steps are the logical process by which
an alcoholic finds and maintains sobriety and becomes
rehabilitated. It has been the history of AA that any
alcoholic who has followed this program without devi-
ation has remained sober. Those who have tried to cut
corners, skip over steps, have eventually found themselves in trouble. This has been the rule rather than the
exception.

"Upon being asked which is the most important of
the Twelve Steps, one of the early members once replied
with another question: 'Which is the most important
spoke of a wheel?' If a wheel has twelve spokes and
one is removed, the wheel will probably continue to
support the vehicle, but it will have lost strength. Removal of another spoke weakens it even more, and
eventually the wheel will collapse. So it is with AA.
Removal of any of the Steps will eventually result in a
collapse.

"It is important that the newcomer be introduced to
the Twelve Steps at as early a date as possible. On these
rules depends his full recovery." [21]

---

21 Anonymous (Evan W.), *A Guide to the Twelve Steps
of Alcoholics Anonymous* (Akron, OH: A.A. of Akron, undated (1945?)) 1.

In June 1946, *The A.A. Grapevine* published an article describing one of the assets and liabilities checklists that was in use at the time. Dr. Bob and many of the A.A. pioneers used these checklists to take newcomers through the Fourth Step.

The list in *The A.A. Grapevine* article contained seventeen assets and seventeen liabilities. This "commercial inventory" is described on page 64 of the "Big Book" as an evaluation of **"the stock-in-trade."** This Moral Inventory has been reprinted and distributed by many of the Intergroup and Central Offices throughout the United States and Canada: [22]

MY DAILY MORAL INVENTORY

LIABILITIES— Watch For:	ASSETS— Strive For:
Self Pity	Self Forgetfulness
Self Justification	Humility
Self Importance	Modesty
Self Condemnation	Self Valuation
Dishonesty	Honesty
Impatience	Patience
Hate	Love
Resentment	Forgiveness
False Pride	Simplicity
Jealousy	Trust
Envy	Generosity
Laziness	Activity
Procrastination	Promptness
Insincerity	Straightforwardness
Negative Thinking	Positive Thinking
Vulgar, Immoral Thinking	Spiritual, Clean Thinking
Criticizing	Look For the Good!

22 Mark W., *The A.A. Grapevine* (New York, NY: The Alcoholic Foundation, Vol. III, No. 1, June 1946) 10

In 1946, Barry C. and Edward W., published *An Interpretation of the Twelve Steps of the Alcoholics Anonymous Program*, which was later renamed *The Little Red Book*. By this time, Barry and Ed had been conducting Beginners' Meetings for almost two years at the Nicollet Group in Minneapolis, Minnesota.

The Author's Note states:

> "The Interpretation of the 12 Steps of the Alcoholics Anonymous program was prepared from a series of notes originally used in Twelve Step discussion meetings for new A.A. members. It proved to be very effective and helpful. Many groups adopted it using mimeographed copies. The demand for the Interpretation in book form from both individuals and groups made printing advisable." [23]

Barry C. and Ed W. continued to publish *The Little Red Book* for the next twenty years. (Hazelden has been publishing a revised version of the book since 1957.) Some of the later Coll-Webb printings included a dust jacket with the following inscription:

> "Few books have a greater record for humble service than *The Little Red Book* upon which so many members have cut their A.A. teeth.

---

23 Anonymous, (Ed W. and Barry C.) *An Interpretation of the Twelve Steps of the Alcoholics Anonymous Program* (Minneapolis, MN: Coll-Webb Company, 1946) 6.

"This book evolved from a series of notes prepared for 12 Step talks to A.A. Beginners. A manuscript drawn up from these notes was sent to Dr. Bob at the request of U.S.A. and Canadian members. He approved the manuscript and the book was published in 1946. . . .

"Thousands of A.A.'s all over the world use *The Little Red Book* as a faithful guide to the working mechanics of the 12 Steps. Based on an orthodox exposition of matter from the book, *Alcoholics Anonymous,* it presents a firm, but workable, evaluation of each step as our founders gave them to us.

"Dr. Bob, co-founder, endorsed the book as 'most helpful.' " [24]

So, Dr. Bob not only authorized the publication of the Akron pamphlet titled *Guide to the Twelve Steps of Alcoholics Anonymous,* he also endorsed *The Little Red Book.* Both publications evolved directly from the A.A. Beginners' Meetings.

Many Beginners' Meetings were closed to alcoholics only. Others were open to **"anyone or everyone seeking a spiritual way of life."** In New York City, the Manhattan Group sponsored both an Open and a Closed meeting. The 1946 meeting list showed that the Closed Beginners' Meeting was held 45 minutes before the Manhattan Group's "regular" Closed Meeting on Thursday night:

---

24 Anonymous, *The Little Red Book* (Minneapolis, MN: Coll-Webb Company, 1954) Back cover of dust jacket.

A.A. Meetings in New York City and Vicinity 1946				
	Group	*Address*	*Type of Meeting*	*Time*
SUNDAY	Manhattan	405 West 41ˢᵗ Street, N.Y.C.	Beginners (Open)	3:00 pm.
THURSDAY	Manhattan	405 West 41ˢᵗ Street, N.Y.C.	Closed (Beginners)	7:45 pm.
THURSDAY	Manhattan	405 West 41ˢᵗ Street, N.Y.C.	Closed (Regular)	8:30 pm. [25]

In September 1947, the Committee for the Southeastern A.A. Convention published the results of a 145-item questionnaire, which had been sent to 185 groups in eleven states from Virginia to Louisiana. Sixty groups answered the questionnaire, which covered the subjects of "Sponsorship," "Twelfth Step Work," "Spiritual Side of A.A.," "Moral Inventory and House Cleaning," and "Education," among others. The responses provide an informative and revealing look into the inner workings of the A.A. fellowship during this time period:

Sponsorship

"The person bringing in the new member is his natural sponsor. If the prospect knows no one in the group, a sponsor is usually appointed until the new member becomes acclimated and has a voice in choosing his own. The duties of the sponsor, although variously expressed, are generally uniform: to acquaint the new member with the A.A. way of life. . . . Practically all

25 Anonymous, *1946 Schedule of A.A. Meetings in New York City and Vicinity* (New York, NY: New York Intergroup Office, 1946) 1

25

groups believe in women sponsors for women, men for men."

Twelfth Step Work

"Practically all groups encourage twelfth step work by new as well as old members, but most suggest that an old member go along if possible. The man who has just dried up a few days is oftentimes closer to the drunk in spirit than one who has been dry for many years.

"Many groups do twelfth step work in asylums, hospitals, jails, penitentiaries, and other institutions. Much work is done in conjunction with the Salvation Army and various Church Missions."

Spiritual Side of AA

"In fifty percent of the groups responding, the subject (of Spiritually) is stressed to new members. Thirty-seven of the sixty groups that replied, discussed the subject (of spiritually) in their educational programs.

"The relative importance of the spiritual phase of the program is well realized as shown by the answers given. Some of them: 'Heart of the Program', 'Utmost Importance', 'Foundation of A.A.', 'Basis of our Success', etc."

Moral Inventory and House Cleaning

"Only two groups (out of 60) require written case histories. In all but four groups, the making of the inventory is left entirely up to the individual, as is also his choice of the other human being on whom he is to unload."

Education

"Only about one half of the groups have a planned educational program for new members. Many have beginners or educational meetings. Materials employed are mainly the A.A. Book and the Twelve Steps." [26]

It is interesting to note that the A.A.'s who summarized the survey results were disappointed to find that **"ONLY"** about one half of the groups sponsored a Beginners' Meeting. These people knew the importance of the "educational" meetings to the overall success of A.A. With this statement, they were in essence, challenging the rest of the groups to start their own Beginners' Meetings.

The Beginners' Meetings in Boston, Massachusetts were a citywide event hosted by the Boston Central Office. The June 1949 meeting list showed that Beginners' Meetings were held at the Central Office at 30 Huntington Avenue, ninety minutes before the All Group Meeting: [27]

---

26 Anonymous, *Digest of Survey on Southeastern A.A. Groups* (Memphis, TN: Memphis Alcoholics Anonymous Foundation, Inc., September 1947) 1-5

27 Anonymous, *List of Groups–Time and Place of Meetings* (Boston, MA: Central Service Committee, June 22, 1949) 1

CENTRAL SERVICE COMMITTEE
ALCOHOLICS ANONYMOUS

30 HUNTINGTON AVENUE, BOSTON 16, MASS.
KEnmore 6-4642

OFFICE HOURS: *9:00 to 5:00 Monday through Friday*
7:00 to 9:00 Wednesday Evenings

List of Groups----Time and Place of Meetings

ALL GROUP MEETING
EVERY WEDNESDAY EVENING AT 8:30 P.M.
30 HUNTINGTON AVENUE

•

BEGINNER'S MEETING
Every Wednesday Evening (7-8 P.M.)
Rooms 204-205----30 Huntington Avenue

The Alcoholic Foundation first published the *Handbook for the Secretary,* in 1950. It was later renamed the *Group Handbook.*

One of the sections contained guidelines for conducting A.A. Meetings. At the time, there were only three types of meetings. These were Open Speaker Meetings, Closed Discussion Meetings, and Beginners' Meetings. The description of a Beginners' Meeting format that was in use in Chicago, Illinois follows:

III. BEGINNERS' MEETINGS

"In larger metropolitan areas a special type of meeting for newcomers to A.A. has proved extremely successful. Usually staged for a half-hour prior to an open meeting, the 'Beginner's Meeting' features an interpretation of A.A., usually by an 'older' member and presented in terms designed to make the program clear to the new member. After the speaker's presentation, the meeting is thrown open to questions. Occasionally the A.A. story is presented by more than one speaker. Emphasis remains exclusively on the newcomer and his problems." [28]

During a taped interview in March 1997, Ennis P. of Miami, Florida recalled how the Beginners' Meetings were conducted in his area. In July 1951, he participated in the "Newcomer Classes," which were held at the local A.A. Club.

Ennis stated that Fred C., the Intergroup Office Manager, established the Beginners' Meetings in Miami. Fred felt it was the responsibility of the Intergroup Office to "get newcomers going in A.A."

Dona H., who later became a South Florida Delegate to the General Service Conference, conducted the initial series of meetings. Ennis stated that Ruth R. was also one of the early instructors.

---

28   Anonymous, *Handbook for the Secretary* (New York, NY: The Alcoholic Foundation, 1950) 2.

In Miami, the Twelve Steps were divided into three classifications. The sessions were taught on three successive Monday evenings at 7:00 P.M.:

Give Up - - - - - - - - - -Steps 1–3
Clean Up - - - - - - - - - -Steps 4–9
Live Up - - - - - - - - - - Steps 10–12 [29]

In addition to the numerous cities already mentioned, the Beginners' Meetings were held in many other locations throughout the United States and Canada. Today, numerous old-timers still talk fervently about taking the Steps and then helping others through them as part of their A.A. service work.

If the Beginners' Meetings were so important, whatever happened to them? Most A.A.'s who have joined the fellowship within the past thirty years have never experienced the miracle of recovery that occurs during the four one-hour sessions.

Ruth R., a Miami Florida old-timer who led the sessions in the mid-1950's, provided some insight into the demise of the Beginners' Meetings. She came into A.A. in 1953. At that time, the two books that were used in South Florida to conduct the meetings were *Alcoholics Anonymous* and *The Little Red Book*.

Ruth recalled that the meetings were discontinued in the late 1950's as the result of the publication of the book, *Twelve Steps and Twelve Traditions* by Alcoholics Anonymous Pub-

---

29 Audio tape interview of Ennis P., conducted by Kevin B., on March 2, 1997

lishing, Inc. In the Miami area, the "Twelve and Twelve" replaced both the "Big Book" and *The Little Red Book*, as "Step Studies" replaced the Beginners' Meetings.

During the process of converting to "Step Studies," the groups extended the period of time for taking the Steps from four weeks to twelve or even sixteen weeks. The laborious and detailed three-column inventory, described on page 65 of the "Big Book," replaced the informal and straightforward assets and liabilities checklist. What had originally been conceived as a very simple program taking a few hours to complete, evolved into a complex and, for many newcomers, an insurmountable barrier to recovery.

"Studying" the Steps is not the same as "taking" the Steps. The "Big Book" states: **"Here are the Steps we took,"** not "here are the Steps we sat around and talked about." The A.A. pioneers have clearly demonstrated that **ACTION**, not self-knowledge, produces the spiritual awakening that results in recovery from alcoholism.

On page 88, the "Big Book" authors write:

"We alcoholics are undisciplined. So we let God discipline us in the simple way we have just outlined.

"But this is not all. There is action and more action. 'Faith without works is dead.' "

—Courtesy of the *NASHVILLE BANNER*

In the early days, the A.A. Beginners' Meetings were an integral part of the recovery process. In these four one-hour sessions, newcomers took ALL Twelve Steps. A majority of them experienced a "transformation of thought and attitude" and never drank again.

Chapter 2

Session #1–Overview and Step 1

There was a period in the history of Alcoholics Anonymous when the program produced a 50 to 75 percent recovery rate from alcoholism. So, how can we get reconnected with this miraculous piece of our glorious past? We need to take a trip back in time. Okay, let's go.

It is the fall of 1946. You have a drinking problem and you telephone Alcoholics Anonymous for help. A.A. responds by sending two people out to see you.

These ex-problem drinkers talk about their personal experiences with alcohol and how they found a way out. They tell you that, as part of their recovery, they try to be of service to others.

After listening to their stories, you agree to be hospitalized. They take you to a local sanitarium where you are withdrawn from alcohol. The process takes three days. During this period of time, you are visited by many of the members of the local A.A. group.

Upon your release, you are assigned a sponsor or sharing partner whose responsibility it is to accompany you to the Alcoholics Anonymous Beginners' Meetings. You take all Twelve Steps in one month. Your life changes — you never drink again.

Sounds incredibly simple, doesn't it? Well, it was simple and it worked! A.A.'s remarkable recovery rate during the

1940's was due, in large part, to these four one-hour sessions. For many thousands of alcoholics, the Beginners' Meetings became **"the foundation stone of (their) recovery."**

So, let's imagine it is early evening on a weeknight in a Midwest city. You are sitting at a table in the meeting room of a local church. You have a copy of the book titled *Alcoholics Anonymous* with you, along with a pencil and paper. The first of the four one-hour sessions is about to begin.

This meeting is hosted by one of the local A.A. groups. The leaders are members of the group who have taken the Steps and have helped others through them. It is now their turn to conduct the Beginners' Meetings.

The only change we've made to this 1946 A.A. meeting format is to use the page numbers from a later edition of the book *Alcoholics Anonymous,* rather than the page numbers from the First Edition, which was in use at that time.

* *

WELCOME to the first of four one-hour A.A. meetings that will change your life! During the next several weeks, you will learn how to recover from the affliction of alcoholism by taking the Twelve Steps as described in the book *Alcoholics Anonymous.*

Alcoholics Anonymous has found an answer to this insidious illness. As members of A.A., we are here to share our solution with you — a spiritually based **"program of action"** that will remove your compulsion to drink and provide you with a new way of living without alcohol.

Our names are _____ and _____, and we are members of Alcoholics Anonymous. We lead these meetings to help insure *our* sobriety. We receive no financial compensation for this service. Our reward is to watch people recover and see them work with others.

We will begin this session by reading a statement from the book *Alcoholics Anonymous:*

> "We are not an organization in the conventional sense of the word. There are no fees or dues what-soever. The only requirement for membership is an honest desire to stop drinking. We are not allied with any particular faith, sect or denomination, nor do we oppose anyone. We simply wish to be helpful to those who are afflicted."
> (*A.A.*, p. xiii, para. 5, line 1; p. xiv, lines 1-6)

The book we are reading from is A.A.'s textbook for recovery. This is the only book we will use during these sessions, except for an occasional reference to an A.A. pamphlet, newsletter article, or source material used to write the "Big Book."

What we just read sums up the A.A. fellowship quite well. We are not a religion, and we don't get involved in politics, psychology or medicine.

As the title of the book implies, we are an anonymous society. You can be assured we will protect your anonymity at this and all other meetings of Alcoholics Anonymous. We ask that you do the same for us and for everyone else who is here tonight.

The "Big Book" was first published in April 1939. It was written by several of the first 100 men to recover from alcoholism. Since then, alcoholics all over the world have used the book as the basis for a program of recovery.

The original title of the "Big Book" was ***One Hundred Men***, because at the time it was written, there were no women on the program. Then, Florence R. started attending meetings in New York City. She stayed sober long enough to convince the men to change the name of the book — which they did. But, because the book was so close to publication, the authors didn't have time to change the contents.

Please keep this in mind as you read the "Big Book." It was written by men for men. Now, of course, there are many women on the A.A. program, but that wasn't the case when the book was first released.

So we can complete each session within an hour and still have ample time for questions, we request that you write down anything you do not understand or need clarified and save it until the end of the session. We will answer questions at that time.

If you cannot find something we say in the "Big Book," consider it to be our point of view rather than fact. We will do our best to keep our personal opinions out of these presentations. We are here to pass on the A.A. program as written and practiced by the early members. We are **NOT** here to provide you with our interpretation of their program.

The Beginners' Meetings began in the early 1940's when A.A. started growing so rapidly it became impossible for the older members to individually take new prospects through the Steps. The sessions were formalized in a September 1944 pamphlet titled *Alcoholics Anonymous–An Interpretation of our Twelve Steps*, published by the Washington, DC Group. Since 1944, this pamphlet has been reprinted throughout the United States. The preface to the pamphlet contains the following:

> "These meetings are held for the purpose of acquainting both the old and new members with the Twelve Steps upon which our program is based.

> "So that all Twelve Steps may be covered in a minimum amount of time, they are divided into four classifications, and one evening each week will be devoted to each of the four subdivisions."
> *(A.A.–An Interpretation of our Twelve Steps*, p. 1)

In 1945, *The Grapevine*, which is a newsletter published by our New York City headquarters, devoted three articles to the Beginners' Meetings. These articles described the sessions in St. Louis, Missouri; Rochester, New York; and St. Paul, Minnesota.

Each group has developed its own guidelines for conducting the Beginners' Meetings. However, all these groups have a common purpose: to provide a safe, structured environment where newcomers learn the principles of A.A., take the Twelve Steps, and have life-changing spiritual experiences. In addition, these meetings give those who have taken the Steps the opportunity to help those who are new to the program.

In order for the process to work, newcomers need to be matched up with A.A. members who are willing to guide them through the four one-hour sessions. Newcomers do not attend Beginners' Meetings alone. They are accompanied by their sponsors or sharing partners.

So that everyone can better understand what is expected of them, we are going to present some of the guidelines for the Beginners' Meetings:

For the Newcomer:

1. Your primary obligation is to attend all four sessions. If you need assistance with transportation, your sponsor or sharing partner will help you make the necessary arrangements.

2. We will read the appropriate parts of the "Big Book" to you, specifically those passages that relate to taking the Twelve Steps.

    If you have brought a "Big Book" and are able to follow along, please do so. We will announce each passage by page number and paragraph before we read it.

    If you don't have a book, we ask that you participate by listening. We will guide you through all Twelve Steps as written by the "Big Book" authors. Please follow their directions, as we read them to you, and you too will recover from alcoholism.

3. Although a written inventory is part of the process, this doesn't mean you have to do the writing. The person who is sponsoring you through

these sessions can help you write your inventory, or he or she can write it for you.

For the Sponsor or Sharing Partner:

1. Your time commitment to the newcomer is approximately four weeks. After that, both you and the newcomer will be expected to assist others through the Twelve Steps.

2. During the next month, call or visit the newcomer frequently to offer encouragement and moral support.

3. Attend the weekly Beginners' Meetings with the newcomer.

4. Offer to help the newcomer with his or her inventory. If necessary, fill out the checklist based on what the newcomer tells you. Keep in mind, the newcomer may not be able to complete the inventory without your help.

5. Share your guidance with the newcomer so he or she can see how two-way prayer is working in your life.

6. Based on your personal experience, answer any questions the newcomer may have about the A.A. program or the A.A. way of life.

It is time to assign sponsors or sharing partners to those who need them. Will the newcomers please stand. These are the people who are here to take the Twelve Steps.

If you have a sponsor or sharing partner that is with you

tonight please be seated. If you don't have a sponsor or sharing partner, or he or she is not at this meeting, please remain standing. We need to assign someone to help you during these sessions.

This is a **WE** program. We attend the Beginners' Meetings together, we read the "Big Book" together, we take the Steps together, and we recover together.

[Ask for volunteers to assist those who are standing.] Thank you. Please be seated. Now that everyone has a sponsor or sharing partner, we can proceed.

Let's start on Roman numeral page 13 (xiii). The first paragraph states:

> *W* E, OF Alcoholics Anonymous, are more than one hundred men and women who have recovered from a seemingly hopeless state of mind and body. To show other alcoholics *precisely how we have recovered* is the main purpose of this book."
> (*A.A.*, p. xiii, para.1, lines 1-5)

So, the "Big Book" authors immediately tell us that the purpose of this book is to show us how to recover from alcoholism. This is a revolutionary statement, because before the "Big Book" was written, there was no hope for alcoholics. Now, anyone who is willing to follow the directions **THEY** have provided, can recover.

This message of hope is expressed again in the third paragraph on page 17:

"The tremendous fact for every one of us is that we have discovered a common solution. We have a way out on which we can absolutely agree, and upon which we can join in brotherly and harmonious action. This is the great news this book carries to those who suffer from alcoholism."
(*A.A.*, p. 17, para. 3, lines 1-6)

In the third paragraph on page 25, the authors explain that, for us, there is no middle ground. We will either find a **"new way of living"** or else succumb to the ravages of alcoholism:

"If you are as seriously alcoholic as we were, we believe there is no middle-of-the-road solution. We were in a position where life was becoming impossible, and if we had passed into the region from which there is no return through human aid, we had but two alternatives: One was to go on to the bitter end, blotting out the consciousness of our intolerable situation as best we could; and the other, to accept spiritual help."
(*A.A.*, p. 25, para. 3, lines 1-8)

In the first paragraph on page 44, the authors describe the alcoholic and then tell us what it is going to take to recover. Starting with the fourth line, they write:

". . . If, when you honestly want to, you find you cannot quit entirely, or if when drinking, you have little control over the amount you take, you are probably alcoholic. If that be the case, you may be suffering from an illness which only a spiritual experience will conquer."

41

(*A.A.*, p. 44, para. 1, lines 4-9)

To make sure everyone understands what we just read, we are going to read the last line again:

"If that be the case, you may be suffering from an illness which ONLY a spiritual experience will conquer."

We now know what we have to do in order to recover from alcoholism. We must undergo a life-changing, spiritual transformation.

We realize this is not the answer many of you expected to find in Alcoholics Anonymous. But, please keep in mind that alcoholism is a fatal illness. Recovery requires **"revolutionary and drastic proposals,"** because prior to A.A., most alcoholics either died drunk or were locked up in jails or insane asylums.

In the second paragraph on page 44, the authors once again inform us of our options:

"To one who feels he is an atheist or agnostic such an experience seems impossible, but to continue as he is means disaster, especially if he is an alcoholic of the hopeless variety. To be doomed to an alcoholic death or to live on a spiritual basis are not always easy alternatives to face."
(*A.A.*, p. 44, para. 2, lines 1-6)

Not only is a spiritual experience possible, it is a guarantee. Just keep an open mind and take the Steps as described in the

"Big Book."

In the third paragraph on page 44, they disclose that, no matter what our present beliefs, there is hope for us:

> "But it isn't so difficult. About half our original fellowship were of exactly that type. At first some of us tried to avoid the issue, hoping against hope we were not true alcoholics. But after a while we had to face the fact that we must find a spiritual basis of life —or else. Perhaps it is going to be that way with you. But cheer up, something like half of us thought we were atheists or agnostics. Our experience shows that you need not be disconcerted."
> (*A.A.*, p. 44, para. 3, lines 1-9)

We find it amazing that the newcomer can start the A.A. program without any specific beliefs or, for that matter, without any beliefs whatsoever. All a person needs is the **"willingness, honesty and open mindedness"** to believe that **WE BELIEVE** this program works.

Let us assure you, we do believe. The Twelve Steps have changed our lives and the lives of countless other alcoholics. This program will change your life too, if you honestly want to recover from this deadly affliction.

Let's see what we can learn about this spiritual solution. In the first paragraph on page 45, the "Big Book" authors state:

> "Lack of power, that was our dilemma. We had to find a power by which we could live, and it had to be

a *Power greater than ourselves.* Obviously. But where and how were we to find this Power?

"Well, that's exactly what this book is about. Its main object is to enable you to find a Power greater than yourself which will solve your problem. That means we have written a book which we believe to be spiritual as well as moral. And it means, of course, that we are going to talk about God."
(*A.A.*, p. 45, para. 1, lines 1-4; para. 2, lines 1-6)

In the second paragraph on page 46, the authors ask us to develop our own concept of God. In other words, they want us to find a God of our understanding:

"Much to our relief, we discovered we did not need to consider another's conception of God. Our own conception, however inadequate, was sufficient to make the approach and to effect a contact with Him. As soon as we admitted the possible existence of a Creative Intelligence, a Spirit of the Universe under-lying the totality of things, we began to be possessed of a new sense of power and direction, provided we took other simple steps. We found that God does not make too hard terms with those who seek Him. To us, the Realm of Spirit is broad, roomy, all inclusive; never exclusive or forbidding to those who earnestly seek. It is open, we believe, to all . . . "
(*A.A.*, p. 46, para. 2, lines 1-13)

The "Big Book" authors have just told us we are going to take some actions that will lead us into the **"realm of the spirit."** Our personalities will change from self-directed to God directed. Our **"attitude and outlook upon life will change"** from **"self-sufficiency"** to **"God-sufficiency."**

As we said earlier, Alcoholics Anonymous is not a religious program. We're free to call this Power by any name we wish, as long as it is a **"Power greater than ourselves."** The "Big Book" authors use many different names for this Power including **"Creative Intelligence," "Universal Mind," "Spirit of the Universe," "Creator,"** and **"Great Reality,"** among others. Quite a few times they call this Power, **"God,"** but they use the word God merely for convenience rather than for any religious purpose. Please refer to this Power by any name you believe in or feel comfortable with.

So, in order to recover from alcoholism, we have to find a **"Power greater than ourselves."** But where are we going to find this Power? The authors answer this question in the second and third paragraphs on page 55:

> "Actually we were fooling ourselves, for deep down in every man, woman, and child, is the fundamental idea of God. It may be obscured by calamity, by pomp, by worship of other things, but in some form or other it is there. For faith in a Power greater than ourselves, and miraculous demonstrations of that power in human lives, are facts as old as man himself.
>
> "We finally saw that faith in some kind of God was a part of our make-up, just as much as the feeling we have for a friend. Sometimes we had to search fearlessly, but He was there. He was as much a fact as we were. We found the Great Reality deep down within us. In the last analysis it is only there that He

may be found."
(*A.A.*, p. 55, para. 2 lines 1-7; para. 3, lines 1-7)

These are dramatic and for some of us revolutionary concepts. Let us summarize them for you. First, the authors of the "Big Book" announce that they have found a way to free us from the bondage of alcoholism. Next, they describe the solution as a **"Power greater than ourselves."** Then, they tell us where to find this Power—right inside each and every one of us.

Now we know **WHERE** to find the Power to overcome our drinking problem. Much of the rest of the "Big Book" is devoted to the question of **HOW** to find the Power.

Basically, we find the Power by taking the Twelve Steps. These Steps are listed on pages 59 and 60. We will now read the Twelve Steps along with the page numbers where each Step is located in the book.

1. *We admitted we were powerless over alcohol— that our lives had become unmanageable.*
   This Step is described on Roman numeral pages 25–32 (xxv–xxxii) and on pages 1–43.
   [The directions for taking Step One are on page 30, paragraph 2, lines 1-3.]

2. *Came to believe that a Power greater than ourselves could restore us to sanity.*
   This Step is described on pages 44–60.
   [The directions for taking Step Two are on page 47, paragraph 2, lines 1-3.]

3. ***Made a decision to turn our will and our lives over to the care of God <u>as we understood Him</u>.***
This Step is described on pages 60–63.
[The directions for taking Step Three are on page 63, paragraph 2, lines 1-8.]

4. ***Made a searching and fearless moral inventory of ourselves.***
This Step is described on pages 63–71.
[The directions for taking Step Four are on page 64, paragraph 1, lines 1-9; paragraph 2, lines 1-6 *(Assets and Liabilities Checklist)*; page 64, paragraph 3, lines 1-2, 6-9 *(Resentments)*; page 68, paragraph 1, lines 1-3 *(Fears)*; and page 69, paragraph 1, lines 1-6 *(Harms)*.]

5. ***Admitted to God, to ourselves, and to another human being the exact nature of our wrongs.***
This Step is described on pages 72–75.
[The directions for taking Step Five are on page 75, paragraph 1, lines 1-4; paragraph 2, lines 1-2.]

6. ***Were entirely ready to have God remove all these defects of character.***
This Step is described on pages 75–76.
[The directions for taking Step Six are on page 76, paragraph 1, lines 3-5.]

7. ***Humbly asked Him to remove our shortcomings.***
This Step is described on page 76.
[The directions for taking Step Seven are on page 76, paragraph 2, lines 1-7.]

8. ***Made a list of all persons we had harmed, and***

became willing to make amends to them all.
This Step is described on page 76.
[The directions for taking Step Eight are on page 76, paragraph 3, lines 2-5.]

9. *Made direct amends to such people wherever possible, except when to do so would injure them or others.*
This Step is described on pages 76–84.
[The directions for taking Step Nine are on page 76, paragraph 3, lines 6-11.]

10. *Continued to take personal inventory and when we were wrong promptly admitted it.*
This Step is described on pages 84–85.
[The directions for taking Step Ten are on page 84, paragraph 2, lines 1-14.]

11. *Sought through prayer and meditation to improve our conscious contact with God as we understood Him, praying only for knowledge of His will for us and the power to carry that out.*
This Step is described on pages 85–88.
[The directions for taking Step Eleven are on page 86, paragraph 1, lines 1-14 *(When We Retire)*; paragraph 2, lines 1-5 *(Upon Awakening)*; page 87, paragraph 3, lines 1-3, page 88, lines 1-7 *(Throughout The Day)*.]

12. *Having had a spiritual awakening as the result of these steps, we tried to carry this message to alcoholics, and to practice these principles in all our affairs.*

This Step is described on pages 89–103 and pages 567-568.

[The directions for taking Step Twelve are on page 89, paragraph 1, lines 4-5.]

(Instructions on how to carry A.A.'s lifesaving message of recovery to others can be found throughout pages 89-103.)

Let's begin with the First Step.

Step 1 *We admitted we were powerless over alcohol—that our lives had become unmanageable.*

Surrender is essential in order to recover from alcoholism. The "Big Book" authors devote 51 pages of the book to the first part of the surrender process, which is to admit we have a problem.

The authors begin by describing the physical and mental symptoms of alcoholism. Later they ask us to acknowledge that we are alcoholics. Before we can do this, we need to know what an alcoholic is.

Much of the first chapter of the "Big Book" is based on two letters written by Dr. William D. Silkworth, a physician at Towns Hospital in New York City. In the late 1930's, very little was known about alcoholism, but much of what Dr. Silkworth wrote then is still relevant today.

In the first paragraph on Roman numeral page 25 (xxv), Dr. Silkworth describes how Bill W., one of the cofounders of Alcoholics Anonymous, recovered from alcoholism. Bill had once been a well respected, Wall Street stock analyst, but he lost everything because of his drinking:

> "In late 1934 I attended a patient who, though he had been a competent businessman of good earning capacity, was an alcoholic of a type I had come to regard as hopeless.
>
> "In the course of his third treatment he acquired certain ideas concerning a possible means of recovery. As part of his rehabilitation he commenced to present his conceptions to other alcoholics, impressing upon them that they must do likewise with still others. This has become the basis of a rapidly growing fellowship of these men and their families. This man and over one hundred others appear to have recovered.
>
> "I personally know scores of cases who were of the type with whom other methods had failed completely."
> (*A.A.*, p. xxv, para. 1, lines 13-26)

For several years prior to 1934, Dr. Silkworth had been treating alcoholics at Towns Hospital with very little success. Then, during his fourth trip to the hospital, Bill discovers the spiritual solution to alcoholism, which he helps develop into the A.A. program.

One of the things Bill is told while in Towns Hospital is that he has to work with other alcoholics in order to stay sober himself. He also learns that alcoholism is a physical and a mental illness, which only a spiritual experience can conquer.

In the first paragraph on Roman numeral page 26 (xxvi), the authors confirm that Dr. Silkworth is well aware of the

50

physical symptoms of alcoholism:

> "The physician who, at our request, gave us this letter, has been kind enough to enlarge upon his views in another statement which follows. In this statement he confirms what we who have suffered alcoholic torture must believe—that the body of the alcoholic is quite as abnormal as his mind. It did not satisfy us to be told that we could not control our drinking just because we were maladjusted to life, that we were in full flight from reality, or were outright mental defectives. These things were true to some extent, in fact, to a considerable extent with some of us. But we are sure that our bodies were sickened as well. In our belief, any picture of the alcoholic which leaves out this physical factor is incomplete."
> (*A.A.*, p. xxvi, para. 1, lines 1-14)

Let's look at this abnormal physical reaction to alcohol. Alcohol is a poison. The normal response to alcohol is to have one or two drinks and stop. But, the alcoholic reaction is much different. We have one or two drinks just to get started.

In the fifth paragraph on Roman numeral page 30 (xxx), Dr. Silkworth tells us that, because of this abnormal reaction, we must refrain from drinking:

> "All these, and many others, have one symptom in common: they cannot start drinking without developing the phenomenon of craving. This phenomenon . . .
> differentiates these people, and sets them apart as a distinct entity. It has never been, by any treatment with which we are familiar, permanently eradicated. The only relief we

have to suggest is entire abstinence."
(*A.A.*, p. xxx, para. 5, lines 1-3, 5-8)

So much for alcoholics ever becoming social drinkers again.

Abstinence might work if alcoholism was only a **PHYS-ICAL** illness, but Dr. Silkworth found that alcoholism has a **MENTAL** component as well. In addition to an abnormal physical reaction, we have a mental obsession. Our mind tells us we are okay, even as alcohol is bringing us closer and closer to death. No matter how much we may want to stop, sooner or later we will return to drinking.

Dr. Silkworth describes this mental obsession on Roman numeral page 28 (xxviii). Please keep in mind Dr. Silkworth is talking about **ALCOHOLICS** when he writes in the fourth paragraph:

> "Men and women drink essentially because they like the effect produced by alcohol. The sensation is so elusive that, while they admit it is injurious, they cannot after a time differentiate the true from the false. To them, their alcoholic life seems the only normal one. They are restless, irritable and discontented, unless they can again experience the sense of ease and comfort which comes at once by taking a few drinks–drinks which they see others taking with impunity."
> (*A.A.*, p. xxviii, para. 4, lines 1-6; p. xxix, lines 1-3)

On page 30, starting with the fourth line in the first paragraph, the "Big Book" authors describe how this mental obsession kills so many of us:

"Therefore, it is not surprising that our drinking careers

have been characterized by countless vain attempts to prove we could drink like other people. The idea that somehow, someday he will control and enjoy his drinking is the great obsession of every abnormal drinker. The persistence of this illusion is astonishing. Many pursue it into the gates of insanity or death."
(*A.A.*, p. 30, para. 1, lines 4-10)

The authors further emphasize the mental obsession in the second paragraph on page 34. They state that, no matter how strong our willpower or conviction, we cannot stop drinking on our own:

"For those who are unable to drink moderately the question is how to stop altogether. We are assuming, of course, that the reader desires to stop. Whether such a person can quit upon a nonspiritual basis depends upon the extent to which he has already lost the power to choose whether he will drink or not. Many of us felt that we had plenty of character. There was a tremendous urge to cease forever. Yet we found it impossible. This is the baffling feature of alcoholism as we know it—this utter inability to leave it alone, no matter how great the necessity or the wish."
(*A.A.*, p. 34, para. 2, lines 1-11)

You see, if our mind didn't deceive us into thinking it's okay to drink, we would never trigger the physical craving for more and more alcohol. So, we have an abnormal reaction of the body and an obsession of the mind, which dooms us to an alcoholic death. On Roman numeral page 29 (xxix), Dr. Silkworth tells us our only hope is a life-changing, conversion experience. Starting with the third line from the top of the page, he writes:

> ". . . After they have succumbed to the desire again, as so many do, and the phenomenon of craving develops, they pass through the well-known stages of a spree, emerging remorseful, with a firm resolution not to drink again. This is repeated over and over, and unless this person can experience an entire psychic change there is very little hope of his recovery."
> (*A.A.*, p. xxix, lines 3-9)

So, a prominent doctor in the field of alcoholism states that the medical community cannot help us. Our only hope is a spiritual awakening.

The next chapter of the "Big Book" deals with Bill W., our New York City cofounder, and how he overcame his alcoholism. Some people have difficulty identifying with Bill because he was such a low-bottom alcoholic. Here, as elsewhere in the book, we ask that you look for similarities rather than differences. See where you can identify with Bill as he continues to use alcohol long after it has become a problem.

In the first seven pages of his story, Bill describes the progressive nature of his drinking. In the 1920's, he was a successful Wall Street stock analyst. In a few short years he loses everything. He becomes an unemployed, hopeless alcoholic.

In the first paragraph on page 8, Bill has a moment of clarity. He realizes he is powerless over alcohol. He is licked — defeated:

> "No words can tell of the loneliness and despair I found in that bitter morass of self-pity. Quicksand stretched around me in all directions. I had met my match. I had been overwhelmed. Alcohol was my master."
>
> (*A.A.*, p. 8, para. 1, lines 1-5)

Bill cannot stop drinking on this admission alone. In late November 1934, an old high school friend, Ebby T., visits him. Bill is drunk. Ebby has been sober for several months. When Bill asks Ebby how he stopped drinking, Ebby tells him, **"I've got religion."** Bill is shocked but he lets Ebby continue because, as he writes, **"my gin would last longer than his preaching."**

But, Ebby doesn't preach to Bill. Instead, he describes a group of people he has recently met who have found a spiritual solution to many of the world's difficulties, including alcoholism. They taught Ebby how to recover from his **"alcoholic illness"** by practicing Four Spiritual Activities–activities that later became the foundation of the A.A. program:

1. **SURRENDER** – A.A.'s First, Second and Third Steps.
2. **SHARING** – A.A.'s Fourth, Fifth, Sixth and Seventh Steps.
3. **RESTITUTION** – A.A.'s Eighth and Ninth Steps.
4. **GUIDANCE** – A.A.'s Tenth, Eleventh and Twelfth Steps.

Soon after Ebby's visit, Bill checks into Towns Hospital. There, under the direction of Dr. Silkworth, Bill is physically withdrawn from alcohol for the fourth time. While in the hospital, Bill applies the Four Spiritual Activities to his drinking problem.

In the second paragraph on page 13, Bill makes a complete **SURRENDER:**

> "There I humbly offered myself to God, as I then understood Him, to do with me as He would. I placed myself unreservedly under His care and direction." (*A.A.*, p. 13, para. 2 lines 1-3)

Immediately after his Surrender, Bill begins **SHARING** his shortcomings with Ebby. Starting with the second line in the second paragraph on page 13, Bill writes:

> ". . . I ruthlessly faced my sins and became willing to have my new found Friend take them away, root and branch. . . .
>
> "My schoolmate visited me, and I fully acquainted him with my problems and deficiencies."
> (*A.A.*, p. 13, para. 2, lines 5-7; para. 3, lines 1-2)

Together, Bill and Ebby identify the blocks that were preventing Bill from tapping into the Power greater than human power–the Power that would solve his problem. Then, starting with the second line in the third paragraph on page 13, Bill learns how to remove the blocks by making **RESTITUTION:**

> ". . . We made a list of people I had hurt or toward whom I felt resentment. I expressed my entire willingness to approach these individuals, admitting my wrong. Never was I to be critical of them. I was to right all such matters

to the utmost of my ability."
(*A.A.*, p. 13, para. 3, lines 2-7)

In the fourth paragraph on page 13, Bill gets quiet, listens to the God of his understanding, and follows **GUIDANCE**. These actions are essential for establishing a two-way relationship with the **"One who has all power"**:

> "I was to test my thinking by the new God-consciousness within. Common sense would thus become uncommon sense. I was to sit quietly when in doubt, asking only for direction and strength to meet my problems as He would have me."
> (*A.A.*, p. 13, para. 4, lines 1-5)

On page 14, starting with the second line in the sixth paragraph, Ebby explains the necessity of working with others:

> ". . . Particularly was it imperative to work with others as he had worked with me. Faith without works was dead, he said. And how appallingly true for the alcoholic! For if an alcoholic failed to perfect and enlarge his spiritual life through work and self-sacrifice for others, he could not survive the certain trials and low spots ahead. If he did not work, he would surely drink again, and if he drank, he would surely die. Then faith would be dead indeed. With us it is just like that."
> (*A.A.*, p. 14, para. 6, lines 2-6; p. 15, lines 1-5)

With Ebby as his guide, Bill takes the Steps and has a sudden conversion experience. He has the **"entire psychic change"**

Dr. Silkworth talks about in his letters.

In the second paragraph on page 14, Bill describes his spiritual awakening:

> "These were revolutionary and drastic proposals, but the moment I fully accepted them, the effect was electric. There was a sense of victory, followed by such a peace and serenity as I had never known. There was utter confidence. I felt lifted up, as though the great clean wind of a mountain top blew through and through. God comes to most men gradually, but His impact on me was sudden and profound."
> (*A.A.*, p. 14, para. 2, lines 1-8)

Bill makes direct contact with the **"Spirit of the Universe"** and recovers from alcoholism. He hasn't had a drink since.

There is additional material within these 51 pages of the "Big Book" that further explains the physical and mental symptoms of alcoholism and how our lives have become unmanageable as the result of our drinking. All we've done is highlight some of the more important passages. However, we hope we've shown you enough for you to proceed.

Now, it's time for us to begin our journey toward the spiritual awakening that will change our lives. Let's see who is ready to take the First Step.

Step 1 *We admitted we were powerless over alcohol— that our lives had become unmanageable*.

The "Big Book" authors tell us exactly what we have to do. In the second paragraph on page 30, they write:

> "We learned that we had to fully concede to our innermost selves that we were alcoholics. This is the first step in recovery. The delusion that we are like other people, or presently may be, has to be smashed." (*A.A.*, p. 30, para. 2, lines 1-4)

In order to smash the delusion that you're not alcoholic, we are going to ask you to answer a simple question, "Are you ready to concede to your innermost self that you are powerless over alcohol?" In other words, "Are you an alcoholic?" All that is required is a "yes" or "no" answer.

If you have reservations about taking the First Step, please let us know. Your sponsor or sharing partner is willing to spend time with you this week to discuss your uncertainty. We want to give you every opportunity to comprehend the devastating consequences of this terrible affliction.

Maybe you don't believe you are an alcoholic. Maybe you think you're here by mistake. We just want you to know we'd rather be inside the fellowship of Alcoholics Anonymous by mistake, than outside the fellowship, drinking and dying by mistake. It's something to think about.

Now, will those who are ready to take the First Step, please stand. This is the First Step question:

"Do you concede to your innermost self that you are an alcoholic?"

Please answer, one at a time, "yes" or "no." After you have answered, please be seated.

[Have each newcomer answer the question.]

Thank you. According to the "Big Book" authors, those who answered "yes" to this question have taken Step One.

That's enough for tonight. In the past hour, we have covered 51 pages of the "Big Book" and taken the First Step. This is a remarkable accomplishment. Congratulations.

Next week we will present Steps Two, Three and Four. We will take the Second and Third Steps during the meeting, and we will provide you with guidelines for taking the Fourth Step. You will share your Fourth Step inventory with another person or persons between the second and the third sessions.

Are there any questions?

Chapter 3

Session #2–Steps 2, 3 and 4

We are about to take our second journey back to the early days of Alcoholics Anonymous — back to the four one-hour Beginners' Meetings of the mid-1940's. During this session we will complete the surrender process we started last week. In addition, we will learn how to identify the shortcomings that have prevented us from establishing an intimate, two-way relationship with the God of our understanding.

* *

WELCOME to session number two of the Alcoholics Anonymous Beginners' Meetings. Together, we are taking the Twelve Steps based on the directions found in the "Big Book" of *Alcoholics Anonymous* and the personal experiences of our A.A. pioneers.

Our names are _____ and _____, and we are members of Alcoholics Anonymous. We are grateful our A.A. Group has asked us to lead these sessions. This is one way we can be of service to others and, at the same time, grow in the **"Fellowship of the Spirit."**

Our goal is to recover from the **"seemingly hopeless state of mind and body"** known as alcoholism. And recover we will. The August 1946 issue of *The A.A. Grapevine* contains an article titled, "Minneapolis Record Indicates that 75% are Successful in A.A." The article demonstrates the importance of the Beginners' Meetings. In Minneapolis, about half of those who stayed on the program for three months recovered from alcoholism. Almost three-fourths of those who remained involved for six months never drank again.

In other areas of the country where Beginners' Meetings are an integral part of the recovery process, we are seeing similar results. We remain involved in the Beginners' Meetings by taking the Twelve Steps, helping others through the Steps, and if possible, leading these sessions. If you participate in the Beginners' Meetings long enough, you **WILL** experience the miracle and you **WILL** recover from alcoholism.

During this session, we'll take Steps Two and Three and establish guidelines for taking the Fourth Step. During the next week, each newcomer is to share his or her inventory with another person or persons.

Older members have told us the only way to understand the "Big Book" is to try to explain it to someone else. They were right. We didn't realize how much we could still learn about our textbook for recovery until we started leading these meetings.

So, we want to thank you for providing us with the opportunity to **"grow in understanding and effectiveness"** by once again taking the Twelve Steps along with you. As we have discovered right here in these Beginners' Meetings, each time we take the Steps, we grow closer to the **"One who has all power."**

Before we begin, we must make sure that the newcomers have someone at this meeting to help them with the Steps. In order for the process to work, sponsors or sharing partners need to accompany the newcomers through these sessions.

Are there any newcomers here tonight who do not have a sponsor or sharing partner with them right now? If so, please stand. [Ask for volunteers to assist those who are standing.] Thank you. Please be seated.

(*Optional: Is there anyone here tonight who didn't have the opportunity to take the First Step last week and would like to do so now? If so, please stand. [Ask the First Step question: **Do you concede to your innermost self that you are an alcoholic?** Please answer, "yes" or "no." After you have answered, please be seated.] Thank you. Those who answered "yes" to this question have taken Step One.*)

As we explained last session, the "Big Book" of *Alcoholics Anonymous* contains step-by-step directions on how to recover from alcoholism by finding and relying upon a **"Power greater than ourselves."** This Power will remove our obsession to drink and lead us to a **"new freedom and a new happiness."**

Let's start with a brief review of what we have learned so far. In the third paragraph on page 64 of the "Big Book," we find an excellent overview of the recovery process. Starting in the middle of the third line, the authors write:

> ". . . for we have been not only mentally and physically ill, we have been spiritually sick. When the spiritual malady is overcome, we straighten out mentally and physically."
> (*A.A.*, p. 64, para. 3, lines 3-6)

63

This is our goal—to overcome the spiritual malady that has separated us from the God of our understanding and doomed us, until now, to the living hell of alcoholism.

How do we overcome this malady? The "Big Book" authors tell us we need to experience a spiritual awakening, which Dr. Silkworth defines as a **"psychic change."** Dr. Silkworth describes the effect of this change on the alcoholic in the first paragraph on Roman numeral page 29 (xxix). There, he states:

> "On the other hand—and strange as this may seem to those who do not understand—once a psychic change has occurred, the very same person who seemed doomed, who had so many problems he despaired of ever solving them, suddenly finds himself easily able to control his desire for alcohol, the only effort necessary being that required to follow a few simple rules."
>
> (*A.A.*, p. xxix, para. 1, lines 1-7)

What are these simple rules? They are, **"Trust in God . . . clean house,"** and **"Help others."** If we follow these guidelines, we will receive the ultimate reward—a spiritual awakening.

Last week we started on our journey to this spiritual awakening by taking Step One. We conceded to our innermost selves we are powerless over alcohol, that is, we are alcoholics.

Will those who have taken Step One, either at the conclusion of last week's Beginners' Meeting or during the week with their sponsor or sharing partner, please stand. (*Optional: Also, will those who took the First Step with us earlier this evening, please stand.*)

Congratulations. Please be seated. We commend you for admitting you have a problem. As the "Big Book" says, **"This is the first step in recovery."** Your admission is a major accomplishment, since most alcoholics live in total denial they have a progressive and fatal illness.

We are now ready to proceed.

Step 2 *Came to believe that a Power greater than ourselves could restore us to sanity.*

Now that we have admitted we are alcoholics, let's look at what else we have to do in order to recover. In the fourth paragraph on page 44, we learn:

> "If a mere code of morals or a better philosophy of life were sufficient to overcome alcoholism, many of us would have recovered long ago. But we found that such codes and philosophies did not save us, no matter how much we tried. We could wish to be moral, we could wish to be philosophically comforted, in fact, we could will these things with all our might, but the needed power wasn't there. Our human resources, as marshalled by the will, were not sufficient; they failed utterly."
> (*A.A.*, p. 44, para. 4, lines 1-2; p. 45, lines 1-8)

What is it going to take for us to find this Power? The answer is in the back of the "Big Book" within Appendix II. Starting with the second paragraph on page 568, we find:

> "Most emphatically we wish to say that any alcoholic capable of honestly facing his problems in the light of our experience can recover, provided he does not close his mind to all spiritual concepts. He can only be defeated by an attitude of intolerance or belligerent denial.
>
> "We find that no one need have difficulty with the spirituality of the program.. *Willingness, honesty and open mindedness are the essentials of recovery. But these are indispensable.*"
> (*A.A.*, p. 568, para. 2, lines 1-5; para. 3, lines 1-4)

The "Big Book" authors maintain that it is our arrogance and shortsightedness that keep us in the dark and block us from the **"sunlight of the Spirit."**

Bill W., our New York City cofounder, had a great deal of difficulty accepting a spiritual solution to his alcoholism. In his story, he explains how he **"came to believe."**

In late November 1934, Ebby T. visits Bill at his Brooklyn, New York home. It is during this visit that Bill first learns about the concept of **"God as you understand God."**

As we mentioned last week, Ebby is one of Bill's high school friends and a former drinking companion. Ebby has been sober for several months. He tells Bill his life has been transformed as the result of practicing the Four Spiritual Activities of Surrender, Sharing, Restitution and Guidance.

Bill is shocked when Ebby starts talking about God. However, he does listen because he realizes Ebby's life has truly changed — Ebby is sober for the first time in many years.

66

Let's pick up the story in the first paragraph on page 12:

> "Despite the living example of my friend there remained in me the vestiges of my old prejudice. The word God still aroused a certain antipathy. When the thought was expressed that there might be a God personal to me this feeling was intensified. I didn't like the idea. I could go for such conceptions as Creative Intelligence, Universal Mind or Spirit of Nature but I resisted the thought of a Czar of the Heavens, however loving His sway might be. I have since talked with scores of men who felt the same way."
> (*A.A.*, p. 12, para. 1 lines 1-10)

Then, Ebby presents Bill with a revolutionary proposition:

> "My friend suggested what then seemed a novel idea. He said, *'Why don't you choose your own conception of God?'*
>
> "That statement hit me hard. It melted the icy intellectual mountain in whose shadow I had lived and shivered many years. I stood in the sunlight at last.
>
> *"It was only a matter of being willing to believe in a Power greater than myself. Nothing more was required of me to make my beginning.* I saw that growth could start from that point. Upon a foundation of complete willingness I might build what I saw in my friend. Would I have it? Of course I would!"
> (*A.A.*, p. 12, para. 2, lines 1-3; para. 3, lines 1-3; para.4, lines 1-6)

Now, let's look at how the "Big Book" authors describe this

"Power greater than ourselves." In the middle of page 46, they ask us to set aside any contempt we may have for spiritual principles and consider our own conception of this Power. If we do, we will be in a much better position to understand the A.A. solution for the alcohol problem. Starting with the third line in the first paragraph, they write:

> ". . . We found that as soon as we were able to lay aside prejudice and express even a willingness to believe in a Power greater than ourselves, we commenced to get results, even though it was impossible for any of us to fully define or comprehend that Power, which is God."
> (*A.A.*, p. 46, para. 1, lines 3-8)

The "Big Book" authors clearly state that it is impossible to define God. We have to stop trying to comprehend this Power with our mind and start accepting this Power with our heart. In the first paragraph on page 47, they explain the concept of **"God as you understand God"**:

> "When, therefore, we speak to you of God, we mean your own conception of God. This applies, too, to other spiritual expressions which you find in this book. Do not let any prejudice you may have against spiritual terms deter you from honestly asking yourself what they mean to you. At the start, this was all we needed to commence spiritual growth, to effect our first conscious relation with God as we understood Him. Afterward, we found ourselves accepting many things which then seemed entirely out of reach. That was growth, but if we wished to grow we had to begin

somewhere. So, we used our own conception, however limited it was."
(*A.A.*, p. 47, para. 1, lines 1-13)

Sometimes we have to take our lives right to the brink of disaster and look death squarely in the eye before we are willing to acknowledge the **"Presence of God."** But there is hope, even for the most stubborn of us. Starting with the seventh line from the top of page 48, the "Big Book" authors maintain that, eventually, most of us become teachable:

" . . . Faced with alcoholic destruction, we soon become as open minded on spiritual matters as we had tried to be on other questions. In this respect alcohol was a great persuader. It finally beat us into a state of reasonableness. Sometimes this was a tedious process; we hope no one else will be prejudiced for as long as some of us were."
(*A.A.*, p. 48, lines 7-13)

In the third paragraph on page 52, the authors make a powerful case for the existence of God:

"When we saw others solve their problems by a simple reliance upon the Spirit of the Universe, we had to stop doubting the power of God. Our ideas did not work. But the God idea did."
(*A.A.*, p. 52, para. 3, lines 1-4)

Once again we need to make a decision. We have to decide whether or not we believe in a Power greater than human power—a **"Spirit of the Universe"**—a God of our understanding.

In the second paragraph on page 53, the "Big Book" authors write:

> "When we became alcoholics, crushed by a self-imposed crisis we could not postpone or evade, we had to fearlessly face the proposition that either God is everything or else He is nothing. God either is, or He isn't. What was our choice to be?"
> (*A.A.*, p. 53, para. 2, lines 1-5)

Now, it's time to choose. Are we willing to concede that there is a **"Power greater than ourselves?"** If we are, we're ready to take the Second Step.

In the second paragraph on page 47, we find the directions:

> "We needed to ask ourselves but one short question. 'Do I now believe, or am I even willing to believe, that there is a Power greater than myself?' As soon as a man can say that he does believe, or is willing to believe, we emphatically assure him that he is on his way. It has been repeatedly proven among us that upon this simple cornerstone a wonderfully effective spiritual structure can be built."
> (*A.A.*, p. 47, para. 2, lines 1-8)

Let's see who is ready to proceed. Will those who have taken Step One please stand. This is the Second Step question:

"Do you now believe, or are you even willing to believe, that there is a Power greater than yourself?"

Please answer, one at a time, "yes" or "no." After you have answered, please be seated.

[Have each newcomer answer the question.]

Thank you. According to the "Big Book" authors, those who answered "yes" to this question have taken Step Two.

Now, let's move on to the Third Step.

Step 3 *Made a decision to turn our will and our lives over to the care of God <u>as we understood Him</u>.*

This Step begins with the third paragraph on page 60. How do we know that? Well, in this case, the "Big Book" authors tell us:

> "Being convinced, *we were at Step Three, . . .*"
> (*A.A.*, p. 60, para. 3, line 1)

Convinced of what? If we've taken the Second Step, we believe that a **"Power greater than ourselves"** can restore us to sanity. But, even though we may believe that the **"Power of God"** is the answer, this doesn't necessarily mean we are willing to accept this solution. In order to recover from alcoholism, we must make a decision to put this Power to work in our lives.

On pages 62 and 63, the "Big Book" authors show us how to become God directed. But, first they disclose how operating on self-will keeps us separated from this **"inner resource."** In the fourth paragraph on page 60, they explain that, when we

71

live on self-will, we are like actors trying to control every detail of a play:

> "The first requirement is that we be convinced that any life run on self-will can hardly be a success. On that basis we are almost always in collision with something or somebody, even though our motives are good. Most people try to live by self-propulsion. Each person is like an actor who wants to run the whole show; is forever trying to arrange the lights, the ballet, the scenery and the rest of the players in his own way."
> (*A.A.*, p. 60, para. 4, lines 1-8)

Does this sound familiar? At one time or another, haven't we all tried to convince those around us they would be much better off if they just did things our way? Attempting to control others is one of the characteristics of selfishness.

In the first paragraph on page 62, the authors declare that it is this selfish, self-centeredness that gets us into trouble. We need to take responsibility for our selfishness and ask God to remove this shortcoming from our lives:

> "Selfishness—self-centeredness! That, we think, is the root of our troubles. Driven by a hundred forms of fear, self-delusion, self-seeking, and self-pity, we step on the toes of our fellows and they retaliate. Sometimes they hurt us, seemingly without provocation, but we invariably find that at some time in the past we have made decisions based on self which later placed us in a position to be hurt.
>
> "So our troubles, we think, are basically of our own

making. They arise out of ourselves, and the alcoholic is an extreme example of self-will run riot, though he usually doesn't think so. Above everything, we alcoholics must be rid of this selfishness. We must, or it kills us! God makes that possible. And there often seems no way of entirely getting rid of self without His aid."
(*A.A.*, p. 62, para. 1, lines 1-8; para. 2, lines 1-8)

Then in the third paragraph on page 62, the authors make clear what happens once we rid ourselves of this selfishness:

"This is the how and why of it. First of all, we had to quit playing God. It didn't work. Next, we decided that hereafter in this drama of life, God was going to be our Director. . . .
Most good ideas are simple, and this concept was the keystone of the new and triumphant arch through which we passed to freedom.

"When we sincerely took such a position, all sorts of remarkable things followed. We had a new Employer. Being all powerful, He provided what we needed, if we kept close to Him and performed His work well."
(*A.A.*, p. 62, para. 3, lines 1-4, 6-8; p. 63, para. 1, lines 1-4)

Now we know our place in God's Universe. Contrary to what we may have thought in the past, the whole world does not revolve around us.

Realizing there is a **"Power greater than ourselves"** is the essence of God Consciousness. As we become aware of the

"realm of the spirit," our lives change. Starting with the fifth line from the top of page 63, the authors explain this awareness:

> "Established on such a footing, we became less and less interested in ourselves, our little plans and designs. More and more we became interested in seeing what we could contribute to life. As we felt new power flow in, as we enjoyed peace of mind, as we discovered we could face life successfully, as we became conscious of His presence, we began to lose our fear of today, tomorrow or the hereafter. We were reborn."
> (*A.A.*, p. 63, para. 1, lines 5-12)

We have been delivered from the gates of hell and have come back to tell what it was like. It isn't a pretty picture. We will never have to **"relive the horrors of the past,"** if we remain in the **"Presence of God."**

It is decision time once again. The "Big Book" authors tell us we are now ready to take the Third Step. In the third paragraph on page 63, they provide us with the directions:

> "We found it very desirable to take this spiritual step with an understanding person, such as our wife, best friend, or spiritual adviser. But it is better to meet God alone than with one who might misunderstand. The wording was, of course, quite optional so long as we expressed the idea, voicing it without reservation. This was only a beginning, though if honestly and humbly made, an effect, sometimes a very great one, was felt at once."
> (*A.A.*, p. 63, para. 3, lines 1-9)

74

We are so fortunate that in the years since the "Big Book" was written the fellowship has grown to where very few, if any, newcomers have to take the Third Step alone. We're here to take this monumental Step with you right now.

Although they say the wording is optional, the authors do provide us with a prayer we can use to take the Third Step. The prayer is in the middle of page 63. Starting with the second line in the second paragraph, it reads:

> ". . . 'God, I offer myself to Thee—to build with me and to do with me as Thou wilt. Relieve me of the bondage of self, that I may better do Thy will. Take away my difficulties, that victory over them may bear witness to those I would help of Thy Power, Thy Love, and Thy Way of life. May I do Thy will always!' "
> (*A.A.*, p. 63, para. 2, lines 2-8)

We would like those who are ready to take the Third Step to read the prayer along with us.

Let's read the Third Step Prayer together.

[Read the prayer a second time.]

Well done! According to the "Big Book" authors, we have taken Step Three.

Even though we've spent a considerable amount of time on the first three Steps, we have only made a series of decisions. Now, we need to take some specific actions that will result in the "personality change sufficient to bring about recovery from alcoholism."

Step 4 *Made a searching and fearless moral inventory of ourselves.*

In the fourth paragraph on page 63, the "Big Book" authors tell us what we need to do now that we've made our decision to proceed:

> "Next we launched out on a course of vigorous action, the first step of which is a personal housecleaning, which many of us had never attempted. Though our decision was a vital and crucial step, it could have little permanent effect unless at once followed by a strenuous effort to face, and to be rid of, the things in ourselves which had been blocking us. Our liquor was but a symptom. So we had to get down to causes and conditions."
> (*A.A.*, p. 63, para. 4, lines 1-2; p. 64, lines 1-7)

Please note the authors say **AT ONCE**. They instruct us to take the Fourth Step immediately after the Third Step prayer. We must overcome those things that have prevented us from tapping into the spiritual solution to our problem.

So, we are now going to establish a direct line of communication with the God of our understanding by eliminating those manifestations of self that have kept us in the depths of loneliness and despair. The "Big Book" authors disclose that liquor is only a symptom of our problem. Sure, alcohol has cut us off from God, but once we stop drinking, we're still separated from the **"One who has all power."** because of our shortcomings. Now, it is time to look at these **"causes and conditions"** by taking an inventory.

The "Big Book" authors start by comparing a personal inventory to a business inventory. In the first paragraph on page 64, they write:

> "Therefore, we started upon a personal inventory. *This was Step Four.* A business which takes no regular inventory usually goes broke. Taking a commercial inventory is a fact-finding and fact-facing process. It is an effort to discover the truth about the stock-in-trade. One object is to disclose damaged or unsalable goods, to get rid of them promptly and without regret."
> (*A.A.*, p. 64, para. 1, lines 1-7)

So, we are going to conduct the equivalent of a commercial inventory on our lives. This implies we are going to look at our assets and liabilities. That's what a commercial inventory is all about. It's an examination of what is working and what is not working in our lives. It allows us to accentuate the positive and eliminate the negative.

Then, in the second paragraph on page 64, the authors clearly explain what we need to do in order to conduct a Fourth Step inventory:

> "We did exactly the same thing with our lives. We took stock honestly. First, we searched out the flaws in our make-up which caused our failure. Being con-

vinced that self, manifested in various ways, was what had defeated us, we considered its common manifestations."
(*A.A.*, p. 64, para. 2, lines 1-6)

Before we get into the details on how to take this Step, we want to emphasize a few things. First, there is no right or wrong way to conduct a Fourth Step inventory. Various assets and liabilities checklists are in use today. You can use any one of them.

Second, the assets and liabilities checklist described on page 64 precedes the three-column inventory shown on page 65. Because this **"commercial inventory"** comes first, we assume the "Big Book" authors are asking us to utilize this simple checklist before attempting the much more difficult example on the following page.

Third, Dr. Bob, our Akron, Ohio cofounder, has been using an assets and liabilities checklist for many years. Dr. Bob believes that, initially, newcomers should be taken through a simplified version of the Steps. Later, they can work the program in more detail.

Dr. Bob takes newcomers through the Steps as quickly as possible. In many instances, he completes the process during the person's three to five-day stay at St. Thomas hospital in Akron, Ohio. Thousands of alcoholics have recovered by following Dr. Bob's "keep it simple" approach.

The "Big Book" authors also urge us to take the Steps quickly. We must discover **"the truth about the stock-in-trade"** in order to remove those behaviors that have cut us off from the **"sunlight of the Spirit."** In the third paragraph on page 65, they provide us with some of the details:

> "We went back through our lives. Nothing counted but thoroughness and honesty. When we were finished we considered it carefully."
> (*A.A.*, p. 65, para.3, lines 1-3)

Please note that the authors ask us to be thorough, and in the very next sentence, they tell us what to do when we are finished. Since this is all in one paragraph, we assume they are asking us to complete this inventory in one sitting.

Keep in mind this is only a suggestion. You can spend as much time on this inventory as you wish, just as long as you and your sponsor or sharing partner complete it before the next session.

Now, let's look at what we put on paper. From pages 64 to 71, the authors present us with a list of liabilities we need to eliminate and assets we need to accentuate.

The liabilities they mention are **RESENTMENT, FEAR, SELFISHNESS, DISHONESTY, INCONSIDERATION, JEALOUSY, SUSPICION,** and **BITTERNESS**. For clarity, we have substituted **FALSE PRIDE** for **INCONSIDERATION, ENVY** for **SUSPICION** and **LAZINESS** for **BITTERNESS**. These liabilities, along with their corresponding assets, are also mentioned in the June 1946 issue of *The A.A. Grapevine.* You can use either the original or our modified "Big Book" liabilities list as a guide for your Fourth Step inventory.

Fourth Step Inventory

Assets and Liabilities Checklist from the "Big Book"
pg. 64:1(1-7); pg. 64:3(1-9); pg. 68:1(1-3); pg. 69:1(1-6:edited)

Liabilities Watch for—		Assets Strive for—
Resentment		Forgiveness
Fear		Faith
Selfishness		Unselfishness
Dishonesty		Honesty
False Pride		Humility
Jealousy		Trust
Envy		Contentment
Laziness		Action

Assets and Liabilities Checklist

We are now going to define these shortcomings in a way that, hopefully, will provide a clearer understanding of their meaning. Let's start with **RESENTMENT**, which is the consequence of being angry or bitter toward someone for an extended period of time over some real or imagined insult. It is a hostile or indignant attitude in response to an alleged affront or personal injury.

FEAR is being afraid of losing something we have or not getting something we want. It manifests itself in many ways such as phobia, terror, panic, anxiety and worry.

SELFISHNESS is concern only for ourselves, our own welfare or pleasure, without regard for, or at the expense of others.

DISHONESTY involves theft or deception. It includes taking things that don't belong to us, cheating people out of what is rightfully theirs, and lying to or withholding the truth from others.

FALSE PRIDE is either feeling better than or less than someone else. Feelings of superiority include prejudice about race, education or religious beliefs, and sarcasm–putting someone else down to make us feel better about ourselves. Feelings of inferiority include self pity, which is excessive concern about our own troubles, and low self-esteem–the lack of self-worth or self-respect.

JEALOUSY has to do with people–being suspicious of another's motives or doubting the faithfulness of a friend.

ENVY has to do with things–wanting someone else's possessions.

LAZINESS means lacking the will or the desire to work. Procrastination, which is postponing or delaying an assigned job or task, is a form of laziness.

Now we now know **WHAT** to inventory. Next, we need to decide **WHO** does the writing. For guidance on this subject, let's look to our New York City cofounder, Bill W.

On page 13, Bill describes the inventory process he went through in one day. Starting with the fifth line in the second paragraph, Bill states:

> ". . . I ruthlessly faced my
> sins and became willing to have my new-found Friend
> take them away, root and branch."
> (*A.A.*, p. 13, para. 2, lines 5-7)

Bill doesn't say, "I ruthlessly wrote down my sins." All he does is acknowledge that he has some shortcomings.

In the third paragraph on page 13, Bill discusses his shortcomings with his sharing partner:

> "My schoolmate visited me, and I fully acquainted
> him with my problems and deficiencies. We made a
> list of people I had hurt or toward whom I felt resent-
> ment."
> (*A.A.*, p. 13, para. 3, lines 1-4)

Here again, Bill doesn't say, "My schoolmate visited me and I read him my inventory." He also doesn't say, "I made a list of people . . . " Rather, Bill writes, **"WE made a list of**

people . . . "

So, together Bill and Ebby made an amends list. Let's think about this for a minute. Bill is in Towns Hospital in December 1934, being withdrawn from alcohol for the fourth time. He is suffering from delirium tremens and is a very sick man. Ebby has been sober for several months. Who do you think did the writing? (It wasn't Bill!)

We are now going to look at the assets and liabilities checklist in more detail. In the third paragraph on page 64, the "Big Book" authors ask us to examine our resentments:

> "Resentment is the 'number one' offender. It destroys more alcoholics than anything else. From it stem all forms of spiritual disease, . . .
>   . . . In dealing with resentments, we set them on paper. We listed people, institutions or principles with whom we were angry."
> (*A.A.*, p. 64, para. 3, lines 1-3, 6-9)

In the first paragraph on page 66, the authors emphasize that our resentments keep us separated from the **"Power greater than ourselves."** We must eliminate them if we are to have a spiritual awakening:

> "It is plain that a life which includes deep resentment leads only to futility and unhappiness. To the precise extent that we permit these, do we squander the hours that might have been worth while. But with the alcoholic, whose hope is the maintenance and growth of a

83

spiritual experience, this business of resentment is infinitely grave. We found that it is fatal. For when harboring such feelings we shut ourselves off from the sunlight of the Spirit. The insanity of alcohol returns and we drink again. And with us, to drink is to die."
(*A.A.*, p. 66, para. 1, lines 1-10)

Then, in the second paragraph on page 67, the authors instruct us to look at our part in each situation to see if we need to make amends:

"Referring to our list again. Putting out of our minds the wrongs others had done, we resolutely looked for our own mistakes. Where had we been selfish, dishonest, self-seeking and frightened? Though a situation had not been entirely our fault, we tried to disregard the other person involved entirely. Where were we to blame? The inventory was ours, not the other man's. When we saw our faults we listed them. We placed them before us in black and white. We admitted our wrongs honestly and were willing to set these matters straight."
(*A.A.*, p. 67, para. 2, lines 1-11)

Let's look at the third sentence again. It reads, **"Where had we been selfish, dishonest, self-seeking and frightened?"** These shortcomings are based on self-will. In addition, they are the opposites of the Four Standards of Honesty, Purity, Unselfishness and Love, which is used as a test for God's will.

Early on, Bill W., Dr. Bob, and other A.A. pioneers learned to test everything they thought, said or did. Now, they are asking us to do the same thing–test our actions. We need to know which path we're on. Are we living in the solution and **"walking hand in hand with the Spirit of the Universe,"** or are we living in the problem and sinking deeper and deeper into **"that bitter morass of self pity?"** It is our selfish, self-centeredness that keeps us blocked from the **"One who has all power"** and prevents us from finding the spiritual solution to our difficulties.

We can use either the A.A. test for self-will or the Four Standards as a test for God's will to determine if we need to make amends:

Test for self-will	Test for God's will
Selfish(ness)	**Unselfishness**
Dishonest(y)	**Honesty**
Self-seeking	**Purity**
Frightened	**Love**

Concerning our resentments, the "Big Book" authors provide us with specific instructions on what to do. We must get beyond them if we **"expect to live long or happily in this world."**

In the third paragraph on page 66, the authors explain that when we hold onto grudges, we are actually allowing others to control our lives.

> "We turned back to our list, for it held the key to the future. We were prepared to look at it from an entirely different angle. We began to see that the world and its people really dominated us. In that state, the wrong-doing of others, fancied or real, had power to

actually kill. How could we escape? We saw that these resentments must be mastered, but how? We could not wish them away any more than alcohol."
(*A.A.*, p. 66, para. 3, lines 1-8)

If we don't deal with our resentments, the future will just be a repeat of the past. Every time we are reminded of an old hurt, the old pain returns and we feel it again and again. In the past we may have drank to numb this pain, but now we are going to take actions to eliminate this pain.

The first thing we do is talk about our resentments with our sponsor or sharing partner. Healing starts with sharing the hurt. But, the healing is not complete until we forgive those who have offended us. We overcome resentment with forgiveness. Therefore, forgiveness is the asset that corresponds to the liability of resentment.

We must change our attitude about the experience. We do this by seeing the source of our pain in a new light. We see the person as a sick individual who needs our prayers not our anger. Whether it is a person who is still in our lives, someone who has passed on, someone we may never see again, or ourselves, the process is the same. Starting with the first line on page 67, the "Big Book" authors write:

"Though we did not like their symptoms and the way these disturbed us, they, like ourselves, were sick too. We asked God to help us show them the same tolerance, pity, and patience that we would cheerfully grant a sick friend. When a person offended we said to ourselves, 'This is a sick man. How can I be helpful to him? God save me from being angry. Thy will be done.'

"We avoid retaliation or argument. We wouldn't treat sick people that way. If we do, we destroy our chance of being helpful. We cannot be helpful to all people, but at least God will show us how to take a kindly and tolerant view of each and every one."
(*A.A.*, p. 67, lines 1-8, para. 1, lines 1-5)

Next, the authors ask us to look at our fears. In the first paragraph on page 68, they write:

"We reviewed our fears thoroughly. We put them on paper, even though we had no resentment in connection with them. We asked ourselves why we had them. Wasn't it because self-reliance failed us? Self-reliance was good as far as it went, but it didn't go far enough. Some of us once had great self-confidence, but it didn't fully solve the fear problem, or any other."
(*A.A.*, p. 68, para. 1, lines 1-7)

If we have faith that God will keep us safe and protected, we will receive the strength and direction to overcome all of our fears. We overcome fear with faith. Therefore, according to the "Big Book" authors, faith is the asset that corresponds to the liability of fear.

In the second and third paragraphs on page 68, they inform us that we will lose our fears if we trust our Creator:

"Perhaps there is a better way—we think so. For we are now on a different basis; the basis of trusting and relying upon God. We trust infinite God rather than our finite selves. We are in the world to play the role He assigns. Just to the extent that we do as we think He would have us, and humbly rely on Him, does He enable us to match calamity with serenity.

" . . . We can laugh at those who think spirituality the way of weakness. Paradoxically, it is the way of strength. The verdict of the ages is that faith means courage. All men of faith have courage. They trust their God. We never apologize for God. Instead we let Him demonstrate, through us, what He can do. We ask Him to remove our fear and direct our attention to what He would have us be. At once, we commence to outgrow fear."
(*A.A.*, p. 68, para. 2, lines 1-7; para. 3, lines 2-10)

In the first paragraph on page 69, the authors mention six additional shortcomings we need to address. They also ask us to make a list of those we have harmed. This will become our amends list—the people to whom we need to make restitution:

"We reviewed our own conduct over the years past. Where had we been selfish, dishonest or inconsiderate? Whom had we hurt? Did we unjustifiably arouse jealousy, suspicion or bitterness? Where were we at fault, what should we have done instead? We got this all down on paper and looked at it."
(*A.A.*, p. 69, para. 1 lines 1-6)

According to the "Big Book" authors, the additional shortcomings we inventory are **SELFISHNESS, DISHONESTY, INCONSIDERATION, JEALOUSY, SUSPICION** and **BIT-**

TERNESS.

So much for the liabilities side of the ledger. Now, what about the assets?

The "Big Book" authors list assets throughout Chapter 5. We've already presented passages that refer to the assets of **FORGIVENESS** and **FAITH**, which are the opposites of **RESENTMENT** and **FEAR**.

Additional assets listed in the "Big Book" and the June 1946 issue of *The A.A. Grapevine* are **UNSELFISHNESS, HONESTY, HUMILITY, TRUST, CONTENTMENT,** and **ACTION.**

We have now looked at both sides of the ledger. Our inventory consists of a list of liabilities to watch for and assets to strive for.

We have completed our presentation of the Fourth Step, but before we end this session, we need to consider one more detail — the person or persons with whom we share our inventory.

Step Five reads: *"**Admitted to God, to ourselves and to another human being the exact nature of our wrongs.**"*

According to the "Big Book" authors, we must discuss our **"problems and deficiencies"** with at least one other person. This individual can be the member of A.A. who is helping you through these sessions, but it doesn't have to be. The "Big Book" authors provide us with other options.

Starting with the fourth paragraph on page 73, they give us directions on how to choose the person or persons with whom we share our inventory. Our sponsor or sharing partner may assist us in putting our checklist together, but we may feel more comfortable sharing the intimate details with a third party. The "Big Book" authors provide us with guidelines regarding the individual or individuals with whom we review our shortcomings:

> "We must be entirely honest with somebody if we expect to live long or happily in this world. Rightly and naturally, we think well before we choose the person or persons with whom to take this intimate and confidential step. Those of us belonging to a religious denomination which requires confession must, and of course, will want to go to the properly appointed authority whose duty it is to receive it. Though we have no religious connection, we may still do well to talk with someone ordained by an established religion. . . .
>
> "If we cannot or would rather not do this, we search our acquaintance for a close-mouthed, understanding friend. Perhaps our doctor or psychologist will be the person."
> (*A.A.*, p. 73, para. 4, line 1; p. 74, lines 1-9; para. 1, lines 1-4)

Therefore, we can discuss our inventory with any number of people. For those who are still uncertain about who to share your checklist with, have your sponsor or sharing partner help you decide.

So, we've explained what needs to be inventoried, who

does the writing, and the person or persons with whom we share our checklist. Now we are going to provide you with an example to illustrate the inventory process.

We have a one-page checklist for you to use. It has the liabilities on the left side and the assets on the right side of the sheet, which is the same format used in the June 1946 issue of *The A.A. Grapevine*. All we have done is remove some of the vertical lines, so the sponsor or sharing partner can list, to the right of the appropriate liabilities, the people, institutions and principles the newcomer needs to talk about.

The first thing the sponsor or sharing partner does is fold the checklist so the assets are hidden from view. Then, he or she asks the newcomer about his or her resentments, by saying, "Who or what are you angry at?" As the newcomer talks about his or her **"grudge list,"** the sponsor or sharing partner puts the names of the people, institutions and principles to the right of the word, **RESENTMENT**.

Keep in mind that it is not necessary to list every resentment the newcomer has ever had in order for the inventory to be thorough. The objective is to get **"to causes and conditions"** and **"get rid of them promptly and without regret."** Sometimes it takes only a few incidents to make clear that **RESENTMENT** has been blocking the newcomer from an intimate, two-way relationship with the **"One who has all power."** Besides, it is more productive to take a few resentments through the entire inventory and restitution process than to list so many resentments that the newcomer becomes overwhelmed and gives up on the process.

It is the pain associated with this **"fact-finding and . . . fact-facing process"** that must be relieved as quickly as possible. Once the newcomer develops confidence and conviction that this course of action will reduce the **"terror, bewilderment, frustration, (and) despair"** associated with living on self-will, he or she will be much more inclined to do additional inventories in the future.

Next, the sponsor or sharing partner asks the newcomer to describe the reasons why he or she is angry and where he or she is at fault. If they both agree that the newcomer needs to make an amends, the sponsor circles the applicable name to the right of **RESENTMENT**.

After the sponsor or sharing partner has compiled the resentment list, he or she moves on to the fear inventory by asking, "Who or what are you afraid of? Let's start with those items for which there is no resentment." After jotting down any names to the right of the word, **FEAR**, the sponsor or sharing partner asks, "Let's revisit your resentment list. Are there any situations where there is both fear and resentment?"

Then the newcomer describes the events surrounding each fearful episode. Once again, the sponsor or sharing partner asks the newcomer to look at **"where were (you) to blame."** If they both agree that the newcomer needs to make an amends, the sponsor circles the relevant name to the right of **FEAR**.

After compiling the **RESENTMENT** and **FEAR** checklists, the sponsor or sharing partner asks the newcomer to consider the remaining items on the liabilities side of the sheet. He or she asks, "Toward whom have you been **SELFISH**?" "Where have you been **DISHONEST**?" "What about **FALSE PRIDE**– do you feel better than or less than others?" "Are you **JEAL- OUS** of any relationship?" "Do you **ENVY** anyone's posses- sions?" "Where have you been **LAZY**?" As each incident comes up, the sponsor or sharing partner adds the name to the right of the specific liability that applies, and, if an amends is agreed upon, he or she circles the appropriate name.

After completing the liabilities side of the checklist, the sponsor or sharing partner unfolds the sheet so that together they can look at the assets side of the ledger. The assets oppo- site the liabilities with the **LEAST** names are the positive char- acteristics that the newcomer already has. Those assets oppo- site the liabilities with the **MOST** names are the qualities that will be strengthened as the newcomer makes the necessary amends.

In our example, the sponsor or sharing partner and the newcomer have put together a list with only a few names to the right of **FALSE PRIDE, JEALOUSY,** and **ENVY** and numerous names to the right of **RESENTMENT, FEAR, SELFISHNESS, DISHONESTY** and **LAZINESS**.

The sponsor or sharing partner summarizes the session by saying, "This inventory shows that, for the most part, you are a humble, trusting, and contented person. In addition, you will become more forgiving, loving, unselfish, honest and industri- ous as you make amends for your resentments, fears, selfish- ness, dishonesty and laziness."

We look at assets as well as liabilities because many of us have lost much of our self-esteem and self-worth as the result of our alcoholism. Even though we've done some very foolish and destructive things while drinking, we will never have to repeat these actions, provided we are willing to admit our faults and correct them. If we are genuinely sorry, God has already forgiven us. Now, it is time to forgive ourselves.

The "Big Book" authors tell us this on page 70. Starting with the fourth line in the first paragraph, they write:

> ". . . If we are sorry for what we have done, and have the honest desire to let God take us to better things, we believe we will be forgiven and will have learned our lesson. If we are not sorry, and our conduct continues to harm others, we are quite sure to drink. We are not theorizing. These are facts out of our experience."
> (*A.A.*, p. 70, para.1, lines 4-10)

So, it is time to make a searching and fearless moral inventory—time to clean up the wreckage of the past so we can experience the **"miracle of healing."** We have copies of our assets and liabilities checklist for those who would like to use this format for their Fourth Step.

As we have already said, there is no right or wrong way to do the Fourth and Fifth Steps. Just do them.

Are there any questions?

Chapter 4

Session #3–Steps 5, 6, 7, 8 and 9

This is the third in a series of four Alcoholics Anonymous Beginners' Meetings. It is the fall of 1946, and we are attending A.A. meetings during which newcomers are taking the Twelve Steps in four one-hour sessions.

For those who are planning to lead these Beginners' Meetings, we want to assure you there are no hard-and-fast rules on how to conduct them. The format we are using is our interpretation of the written and oral histories of old-timers who attended and led these meetings in the 1940's. Please feel free to modify or adapt this format to fit your specific needs, but keep in mind the closer you stay to the "original" program the closer you'll get to the extraordinary success of A.A.'s early days.

* *

WELCOME to session number three of the A.A. Beginners' Meetings. Together, we're taking the Twelve Steps as described in the "Big Book" of *Alcoholics Anonymous.* Our objective is to make conscious contact with the Power greater than human power that will free us from the deadly affliction of alcoholism.

Our names are _____ and _____, and we are members of Alcoholics Anonymous. We're here to guide you on your journey toward a spiritual solution to your drinking problem.

In the last two weeks, we have taken Steps One through Four. Hopefully, during the past week, each newcomer has taken the Fifth Step with his or her sponsor or sharing partner.

(**Optional:** *Are there any newcomers here tonight who do not have a sponsor or sharing partner with them right now? If so, please stand. We need to assign someone to help you during these sessions. [Ask for volunteers to assist those who are standing.] Thank you. Please be seated.*)

Let's see who is on track — "on the beam" as some of us like to say. Will those who have shared a Fourth Step inventory with another person or persons, please stand.

Congratulations, please be seated. We commend you for having the **"willingness, honesty and open mindedness"** to do what is necessary to recover from alcoholism.

You are well on your way to that promised spiritual awakening. We want you to know that everything you read and hear tonight is for your benefit. You've done the work — now you will receive the rewards.

As we said last week, we don't care who did the writing, just as long as you and your sponsor or sharing partner came up with a list of shortcomings and a list of individuals and organizations to whom you need to make amends. You will turn over your shortcomings to the God of your understanding in Steps Six and Seven and make restitution to those you've harmed in Steps Eight and Nine.

We are entering the phase of the program where more and

more actions are required. These actions produce results. Many of these results are in the form of promises which, as our lives change, become an integral part of our spiritual being.

If our lives didn't get better, why would we want to stay sober? If all we had to look forward to was restlessness, irritability and discontentment, why do the work? A.A. offers so much more than just freedom from alcohol. We have found a new way of living far more beautiful than anything we ever could have imagined. That's why we take the Steps, and that's why we take them again and again.

Before we move on to Steps Six, Seven, Eight and Nine, let's review what the "Big Book" authors have to say about the Fifth Step. This is the Step during which God reveals to us, with the help of another person, the shortcomings that have been blocking us from the **"sunlight of the Spirit."**

Step 5 *Admitted to God, to ourselves, and to another human being the exact nature of our wrongs.*

On page 72, starting with the ninth line in the second paragraph, the "Big Book" authors tell us why we need to admit our liabilities to another person:

> ". . . The best reason first: If we skip this vital step, we may not overcome drinking. Time after time newcomers have tried to keep to themselves certain facts about their lives. Trying to avoid this humbling experience, they have turned to easier methods. Almost invariably they got drunk. Having persevered with

97

the rest of the program, they wondered why they fell. We think the reason is that they never completed their housecleaning. They took inventory all right, but hung on to some of the worst items in stock. They only *thought* they had lost their egoism and fear; they only *thought* they had humbled themselves. But they had not learned enough of humility, fearlessness and honesty, in the sense we find it necessary, until they told someone else *all* their life story."
(*A.A.*, p. 72, para. 2, lines 9-13; p. 73, lines 1-10)

Once again, the "Big Book" authors instruct us to take "stock," in other words, to conduct a commercial inventory of our life. They ask us to look at the assets of **HUMILITY, FEARLESSNESS** and **HONESTY** and the liabilities of **EGOISM** and **FEAR.**

We share our inventory because we are great at self deception. Aren't we the ones who used to say we didn't have a drinking problem? Didn't we tell ourselves over and over that we were doing fine as we were sinking deeper and deeper into the abyss of alcoholism?

Since we're not good judges of character, especially our own, we confide in someone else. Only another person can see us as we really are.

As we explained last week, we can share our checklist with any number of people. Some of those mentioned on page 74 of the "Big Book" are church leaders, doctors, psychologists and friends.

The person we choose has to be closemouthed, trustworthy

and supportive. He or she must never discuss our inventory with a third party. On page 74, starting with the seventh line in the second paragraph, the "Big Book" authors write:

> ". . . It is important that he be able to keep a confidence; that he fully understand and approve what we are driving at; that he will not try to change our plan."
> (*A.A.*, p. 74, para. 2, lines 7-9; p. 75, line 1)

The authors give us specific instructions for taking the Fifth Step. In the first paragraph on page 75, they tell us to take action immediately:

> "When we decide who is to hear our story, we waste no time. We have a written inventory and we are prepared for a long talk. We explain to our partner what we are about to do and why we have to do it. He should realize that we are engaged upon a life-and-death errand. Most people approached in this way will be glad to help; they will be honored by our confidence."
> (*A.A.*, p. 75, para. 1, lines 1-8)

In the second paragraph on page 75, they provide us with additional directions:

> "We pocket our pride and go to it, illuminating every twist of character, every dark cranny of the past."
> (*A.A.*, p. 75, para. 2, lines 1-2)

Then, the "Big Book" authors announce that, once we admit our shortcomings, our lives will change. We begin to experi-

Fourth Step Inventory

Assets and Liabilities Checklist from the "Big Book"
pg. 64:1(1-7); pg. 64:3(1-9); pg. 68:1(1-3); pg. 69:1(1-6:edited)

Liabilities Watch for—					Assets Strive for—
Resentment	Ex	Myself	Court	God	Forgiveness
Fear	Court	Relapse	Health		Faith
Selfishness	Ex	Employer	(Friend #1)		Unselfishness
Dishonesty	(Ex)	Myself	(Employer)	(Friend #2)	Honesty
False Pride	God	Employer			Humility
Jealousy	(Family Member)				Trust
Envy					Contentment
Laziness	(Ex)	Employer	(Myself)		Action
Shame	Friend #2				Self-respect

Example of Assets and Liabilities Checklist with Eight Step Amends List

ence a **"transformation of thought and attitude."** On page 75, starting with the second line in the second paragraph, they describe some of these changes:

> ". . .Once we have taken this step, withholding nothing, we are delighted. We can look the world in the eye. We can be alone at perfect peace and ease. Our fears fall from us. We begin to feel the nearness of our Creator. We may have had certain spiritual beliefs, but now we begin to have a spiritual experience. The feeling that the drink problem has disappeared will often come strongly. We feel we are on the Broad Highway, walking hand in hand with the Spirit of the Universe." (*A.A.*, p. 75, para. 2, lines 2-11)

We are well on our way toward recovering from alcoholism. The authors state that we are in the process of having a spiritual experience and, as a result, our obsession to drink is being removed.

It is now time to ask the God of our understanding to remove the blocks we identified in Steps Four and Five. Let's proceed to the Sixth Step.

Step 6 *Were entirely ready to have God remove all these defects of character.*

In this Step, the "Big Book" authors have us answer a simple question. On page 76, starting with the third line in the first paragraph, they ask:

101

> ". . . Are we now ready to let God remove
> from us all the things which we have admitted are ob-
> jectionable? Can He now take them all—every one?
> If we still cling to something we will not let go, we
> ask God to help us be willing."
> (*A.A.*, p. 76, para. 1, lines 3-7)

So, according to the "Big Book" authors, it is decision time once again. We realize they want you to take your Sixth Step on the same evening you share your Fourth Step with your sponsor or sharing partner. In case he or she didn't take you through the Sixth Step, we'll take you through it now. If you have already taken the Sixth Step, we ask that you take it again now with the Group.

During the Fifth Step, we identified our liabilities using one of the checklists we described last week. In the Sixth Step, we make the preparations necessary to turn these shortcomings over to the God of our understanding.

Let's start with a moment of silence so we can ask God to remove the liabilities that we found were blocking us when we shared our inventory. These are the items on the left side of our assets and liabilities checklist that have marks to the right of them. If we are still holding on to some of these shortcomings, we pray for the willingness to let go of them.

(Observe one to two minutes of silence.)

Now, will those who have taken Steps One through Five please stand. This is the Sixth Step question:

"Are you now ready to let God remove from you all the things which you have admitted are objectionable?"

Please answer, one at a time, "yes" or "no." After you have answered, please be seated.

[Have each newcomer answer the question.]

Thank you.

According to the "Big Book" authors, those who answered "yes" to this question have taken Step Six and are ready to move on to the Seventh Step.

Step 7 *Humbly asked Him to remove our shortcomings.*

This Step is straightforward. It consists of a prayer in which we ask God to remove our liabilities and strengthen our assets so we can be of maximum service to all.

This prayer is found in the second paragraph on page 76. It reads:

> "... 'My Creator, I am now willing that you should have all of me, good and bad. I pray that you now remove from me every single defect of character which stands in the way of my usefulness to you and my fellows. Grant me strength, as I go out from here, to do your bidding. Amen.' "

(*A.A.*, p. 76, para. 2, lines 1-7)

We would like those who are ready to take the Seventh Step to read the prayer along with us.

Let's read the Seventh Step Prayer together.

[Read the prayer a second time.]

According to the "Big Book" authors, we have taken Step Seven.

Now, it is time to clear away the wreckage of our past. We do this by making amends or restitution.

Step 8 *Made a list of all persons we had harmed, and became willing to make amends to them all.*

The "Big Book" authors state, **"made a list."** Do we need to make this list? Actually, no! We compiled our list as part of our Fourth Step. In the third paragraph on page 76, they confirm this:

> "Now we need more action, without which we find that 'Faith without works is dead.' Let's look at *Steps Eight and Nine*. We have a list of all persons we have harmed and to whom we are willing to make amends. We made it when we took inventory."
> (*A.A.*, p. 76, para. 3, lines 1-5)

That's why we hold onto our Fourth Step inventory. It

contains our Eighth Step amends list. Referring to our assets and liabilities checklist, our amends are the names at the top of the page that have one or more marks under them.

We congratulate those who came up with a list of individuals and organizations to whom you are willing to make amends. According to the "Big Book" authors, you have taken Step Eight.

Let's move on to the Ninth Step.

Step 9 *Made direct amends to such people, wherever possible, except when to do so would injure them or others.*

The amends process is explained in detail on pages 76 through 83. On page 76, starting with the sixth line in the third paragraph, the "Big Book" authors tell us what we need to do:

> ". . . Now we go out to our fellows and repair the damage done in the past. We attempt to sweep away the debris which has accumulated out of our effort to live on self-will and run the show ourselves. If we haven't the will to do this, we ask until it comes. Remember it was agreed at the beginning *we would go to any lengths for victory over alcohol.*"
> (*A.A.*, p. 76, para. 3, lines 6-13)

We may be hesitant to make amends to those who are still upset with us or suspicious of our motives. In the fourth paragraph on page 76, the authors provide us with guidelines on how to approach these individuals:

> "Probably there are still some misgivings. As we look over the list of business acquaintances and friends we have hurt, we may feel diffident about going to some of them on a spiritual basis. Let us be reassured. To some people we need not, and probably should not emphasize the spiritual feature on our first approach. We might prejudice them. At the moment we are trying to put our lives in order. But this is not an end in itself. Our real purpose is to fit ourselves to be of maximum service to God and the people about us."
> (*A.A.*, p. 76, para. 4, lines 1-6; p. 77, lines 1-4)

In the last sentence of this paragraph, the authors explicitly state our purpose for living. They maintain that we are here to serve God and our fellows.

Then, on page 77 the "Big Book" authors ask us to let our actions, rather than our words, demonstrate that we have changed. Starting with the fourth line from the top of the page, they write:

> ". . . It is seldom wise to approach an individual, who still smarts from our injustice to him, and announce that we have gone religious. In the prize ring, this would be called leading with the chin. Why lay ourselves open to being branded fanatics or religious bores? We may kill a future opportunity to carry a beneficial message. But our man is sure to be impressed with a

sincere desire to set right the wrong. He is going to be more interested in a demonstration of good will than in our talk of spiritual discoveries."
(*A.A.*, p. 77, lines 4-14)

One of the most difficult amends to make is to someone we genuinely don't like. But, whether we like the person or not, we must proceed. On page 77, starting with the ninth line in the first paragraph, we find:

". . . Nevertheless, with a person we dislike, we take the bit in our teeth. It is harder to go to an enemy than to a friend, but we find it much more beneficial to us. We go to him in a helpful and forgiving spirit, confessing our former ill feeling and expressing our regret."
(*A.A.*, p. 77, para. 1, lines 9-14)

In the second paragraph on page 77, the "Big Book" authors even provide us with instructions on what to say:

"Under no condition do we criticize such a person or argue. Simply we tell him that we will never get over drinking until we have done our utmost to straighten out the past. We are there to sweep off our side of the street, realizing that nothing worth while can be accomplished until we do so, never trying to tell him what he should do. His faults are not discussed. We stick to our own. If our manner is calm, frank, and open, we will be gratified with the result."
(*A.A.*, p. 77, para. 2, lines 1-5; p. 78, lines 1-4)

The authors make it clear what we are to do about our debts, which is to pay them. We may not like the sacrifice required to make good on our bills, but sacrifice we must. The process forces us to rely on God for the strength and courage to make good on **"past misdeeds."** Under God's direction, we find it much easier to make restitution than we ever thought possible. In the second paragraph on page 78, they state:

> "Most alcoholics owe money. We do not dodge our creditors. Telling them what we are trying to do, we make no bones about our drinking; they usually know it anyway, whether we think so or not. Nor are we afraid of disclosing our alcoholism on the theory it may cause financial harm. Approached in this way, the most ruthless creditor will sometimes surprise us. Arranging the best deal we can we let these people know we are sorry. Our drinking has made us slow to pay. We must lose our fear of creditors no matter how far we have to go, for we are liable to drink if we are afraid to face them."
> (*A.A.*, p. 78, para. 2, lines 1-12)

Keep in mind that courage is not the absence of fear. Courage is facing the fear and walking through it.

In the first paragraph on page 79, the "Big Book" authors instruct us to let the God of our understanding be our guide. This reliance upon God is essential, if we are to outgrow the fears that have separated us from the **"One who has all power"**:

> "Although these reparations take innumerable forms, there are some general principles which we find guid-

ing. Reminding ourselves that we have decided to go to any lengths to find a spiritual experience, we ask that we be given strength and direction to do the right thing, no matter what the personal consequences may be. We may lose our position or reputation or face jail, but we are willing. We have to be. We must not shrink at anything."
(*A.A.*, p. 79, para. 2, lines 1-9)

The authors suggest we ask others for help before we make some of our more difficult amends. We need direction, preferably from someone who understands the inventory and restitution process. In the first paragraph on page 80, they caution us not to create further harm as we clean up our side of the street:

"Before taking drastic action which might implicate other people we secure their consent. If we have obtained permission, have consulted with others, asked God to help and the drastic step is indicated we must not shrink."
(*A.A.*, p. 80, para. 1, lines 1-5)

In the first paragraph on page 82, we are again advised to seek God's aid as we make good on our past misdeeds:

"Perhaps there are some cases where the utmost frankness is demanded. No outsider can appraise such an intimate situation. It may be that both will decide that the way of good sense and loving kindness is to let by-gones be by-gones. Each might pray about it, having the other one's happiness uppermost in mind."

(*A.A.*, p. 82, para.1, lines 1-6)

This is an example of how we must be tactful and consid-erate of others as we make our amends. No one said it would be easy — it just has to be done.

On page 82, starting with the second line in the second para-graph, the "Big Book" authors emphatically state that **STOP-PING DRINKING IS ONLY THE BEGINNING.** We must take additional actions if we are to recover from alcoholism:

> ". . . Sometimes we hear an alcoholic say that the only thing he needs to do is to keep sober. Certainly he must keep sober, for there will be no home if he doesn't. But he is yet a long way from making good to the wife or parents whom for years he has so shockingly treated. . . .
>
> "The alcoholic is like a tornado roaring his way through the lives of others. Hearts are broken. Sweet relationships are dead. Affections have been uprooted. Selfish and inconsiderate habits have kept the home in turmoil. We feel a man is unthinking when he says that sobriety is enough."
> (*A.A.*, p. 82, para. 2, lines 2-7; para. 3, lines 1-6)

NOT DRINKING IS NOT ENOUGH. The authors make that perfectly clear. Starting with the first paragraph on page 83, they write:

> "Yes, there is a long period of reconstruction ahead. We must take the lead. A remorseful mumbling that we are sorry won't fill the bill at all. We ought to sit

down with the family and frankly analyze the past as
we now see it, being very careful not to criticize them.
Their defects may be glaring, but the chances are that
our own actions are partly responsible. So we clean
house with the family, asking each morning in meditation that our Creator show us the way of patience,
tolerance, kindliness and love.

"The spiritual life is not a theory. *We have to live it.*"
(*A.A.*, p. 83, para. 1, lines 1-10; para. 2, line 1)

Here we are told that, in order to recover from alcoholism,
we have to live the A.A. program. So, we don't just take the
Steps, we **LIVE** the Steps on a daily basis.

In the third paragraph on page 83, the "Big Book" authors
give us directions on what to do if we can't make amends to
someone face-to-face:

"There may be some wrongs we can never fully right.
We don't worry about them if we can honestly say to
ourselves that we would right them if we could.
Some people cannot be seen—we send them an honest
letter."
(*A.A.*, p. 83, para. 3, lines 1-5)

The authors conclude the Ninth Step with another list of
benefits. On page 83, starting with the fourth paragraph, they
tell us precisely what is going to happen once we commence to
clear away the wreckage of our past. They describe these benefits as promises. The "Big Book" is filled with promises. These
are just a few of them:

"If we are painstaking about this phase of our development, we will be amazed before we are half way through. We are going to know a new freedom and a new happiness. We will not regret the past nor wish to shut the door on it. We will comprehend the word serenity and we will know peace. No matter how far down the scale we have gone, we will see how our experience can benefit others. That feeling of uselessness and self-pity will disappear. We will lose interest in selfish things and gain interest in our fellows. Self-seeking will slip away. Our whole attitude and outlook upon life will change. Fear of people and of economic insecurity will leave us. We will intuitively know how to handle situations which used to baffle us. We will suddenly realize that God is doing for us what we could not do for ourselves."
(*A.A.*, p. 83, para. 4, lines 1-5; p. 84, lines 1-11)

What a message of hope! It is almost beyond comprehension that all of these wonderful events will **"come to pass"** if we just make amends to those whom we have harmed. But, they will happen — that's a guarantee.

Dr. Bob, our Akron, Ohio cofounder, learned that he could not stay sober until he made his amends. He accomplished this in one day. On page 156, starting with the first paragraph, we read about Dr. Bob's Ninth Step:

"One morning he took the bull by the horns and set out to tell those he feared what his trouble had been. He found himself surprisingly well received, and learned that many knew of his drinking. Stepping

112

into his car, he made the rounds of people he had hurt. He trembled as he went about, for this might mean ruin, particularly to a person in his line of business.

"At midnight he came home exhausted, but very happy. He has not had a drink since."
(*A.A.*, p. 156, para. 1, lines 1-8; para. 2, lines 1-2)

This concludes our presentation of Step Nine. For the newcomer, part of your assignment for the next week is to start making amends to those on your list. If you are not sure how to proceed with a specific amends, ask your sponsor or sharing partner for help.

Next week, we will take Steps Ten, Eleven and Twelve. But, before we end this session, we need to lay the groundwork for the Eleventh Step. This is the Step that puts us in direct contact with the spiritual solution to our drinking problem.

Step Eleven reads: *"Sought through prayer and meditation to improve our conscious contact with God __as we understood Him__, praying only for knowledge of His will for us and the power to carry that out."*

Many A.A.'s refer to **"prayer and meditation"** as two-way prayer. Prayer is talking to God, and meditation is listening to God. We listen in order to receive guidance from the One **"who has all knowledge and power."**

The "Big Book" authors have been preparing us for this

conscious contact with the God of our understanding by interspersing references about two-way prayer throughout the book. So, before we look ahead to the Eleventh Step, we're going to look back at some of the previous "Big Book" passages that refer to guidance.

Let's start by defining "guidance." The dictionary tells us that "to guide" means to lead, direct, influence, or regulate. Two synonyms are to disclose and to show.

When we look in the "Big Book" for passages that refer to guidance, we find there are at least eighteen of them. We just read one of them a few minutes ago. Let's go back to page 83 and reexamine the last sentence in the first paragraph:

> ". . . So we clean house with the family, asking each morning in meditation that our Creator **SHOW** us the way of patience, tolerance, kindliness and love."
> (*A.A.*, p. 83, para. 1, lines 7-10)

In this passage, the "Big Book" authors instruct us to conduct a daily "quiet time." It is during this period of meditation that God will **SHOW** us–in other words, God will guide us–to a new way of living based on the assets of **PATIENCE, TOLERANCE, KINDLINESS** and **LOVE.**

There are many more references to guidance, starting all the way back at the First Step. We're only going to mention a few of them.

On page 13 in "Bill's Story," our New York City cofounder

writes about **"prayer and meditation."** Starting with the third line in the fourth paragraph, Bill explains:

> ". . . I was to sit quietly when in doubt, asking only for **DIRECTION** and strength to meet my problems as He would have me."
> (*A.A.*, p. 13, para. 4, lines 3-5)

When we ask God for **DIRECTION** and strength, we are calling upon the **"Spirit of the Universe"** for the guidance and power to overcome our difficulties. In other words, "When God guides, God provides."

It is essential that we **"sit quietly,"** especially during periods of stress or uncertainty, so we can clearly hear what God has to say. Meditation is based on the belief that God speaks to those who are willing to listen. We write down the thoughts and ideas we receive so we can separate and take action on the guidance that comes from **"infinite God rather than our finite selves."**

How do we determine the source of our guidance? We use the test we described last week, which is the A.A. test for self-will. The "Big Book" authors show us how to use this test three times. In the Fourth Step we apply the test in connection with our assets and liabilities checklist to determine if we need to make amends. We also use this test in our Tenth and Eleventh Steps.

Let's look again at how the authors use the A.A. test for self-will in the Fourth Step:

Test for self-will	Test for God's will
Selfish(ness)	**Unselfishness**
Dishonest(y)	**Honesty**
Self-seeking	**Purity**
Frightened	**Love**

We use essentially the same test to examine what we put on paper during our "quiet time." If what we have written is honest, pure, unselfish **AND** loving, we can conclude that this guidance is in keeping with God's will for us. If what we have written is dishonest, resentful, selfish **OR** fearful, we can assume this guidance is based on self-will rather than God's will. We take action only on the guidance that passes all four elements of the test for God's will.

On page 57, starting with the third line in the second paragraph, the "Big Book" authors state that God **"is constantly being revealed"** to us:

> ". . . He has come to all who have honestly sought Him.
>
> "When we drew near to Him He **DISCLOSED** Himself to us!"
>
> (*A.A.*, p. 57, para. 2, lines 3-4; para. 3, lines 1-2)

When we seek God's guidance, we find a **"new power, peace, happiness and . . . direction"** beyond our wildest dreams. As we will learn next week, our Creator speaks directly to us through **"inspiration, an intuitive thought, or a decision."**

On page 69, starting with the sixth line in the third paragraph, we find another reference to two-way prayer:

> ". . . In meditation, we ask God what we should do about each specific matter. The right answer will come, if we want it."
> (*A.A.*, p. 69, para. 3, lines 6-8)

When we ask specific questions, we receive specific answers. In the second paragraph on page 70, we are told what to ask for:

> ". . . We earnestly pray for the right ideal, for **GUIDANCE** in each questionable situation, for sanity, and for the strength to do the right thing."
> (*A.A.*, pg. 70, para. 2, lines 1-4)

These are just a few examples from the "Big Book" on **"prayer and meditation."** They are sufficient to get us started. We now know what we need to do in order to live in the **"realm of the spirit."**

We're going to provide you with some additional material on how to establish a conscious contact with the God of your understanding. In the late 1930's, a friend of Dr. Bob's wrote a short essay titled, **"How to Listen to God."** It is one of the clearest set of instructions we have found on how to practice the Eleventh Step.

We will briefly take you through this four-page pamphlet. It contains universal spiritual principles that can be applied by **"anyone or everyone interested in a spiritual way of life."** We suggest you conduct your daily meditation based on these guidelines. Next session, let us know what happened.

In the opening paragraphs, the author states that **"prayer and meditation"** will change our lives:

> "These are a few simple suggestions for people who are willing to make an experiment. You can discover for yourself the most important and practical thing any human being can ever learn—how to be in touch with God."

> "All that is needed is the ***willingness to try it honestly****. Every person who has done this consistently and sincerely has found that it really works."
> ("How to Listen to God," p. 1)

We have found that two-way prayer **"works, if we have the proper attitude and work at it."** With time and practice, it will **"gradually become a working part of the mind."**

At the bottom of the first page, the author provides us with directions for conducting a "quiet time":

> "Anyone can be in touch with God, anywhere and at any time, ***if the conditions are obeyed***.

> "These are the conditions:

> > – to be quiet and still;
> > – to listen;
> > – to be honest about every thought that comes;
> > – to test the thoughts to be sure they come from God;
> > – to obey."

("How to Listen to God," p. 1)

Within the remaining pages of the pamphlet, the author explains each of these conditions in detail. In the middle of the second page, he encourages us to record our thoughts and ideas:

Write!
"Here is the important key to the whole process. Write down everything that comes into your mind. ***Every-thing.*** Writing is simply a means of recording so that you can remember later."
("How to Listen to God," p. 2)

On the third page, he explains how to distinguish between God directed and self-directed guidance:

Test
". . . Take a good look at what you have written. ***Not every thought we have comes from God.*** So we need to test our thoughts. Here is where the written record helps us to be able to look at them.

 a) Are these thoughts completely ***honest, pure, unselfish and loving?***
 b) Are these thoughts in line with our duties to our family—to our community?
 c) Are these thoughts in line with our understanding of the teachings found in our spiritual literature?"
("How to Listen to God," p. 3)

The author of the pamphlet asks us to test our guidance using the Four Standards of Honesty, Purity, Unselfishness and

Love. This test will help us determine if what we have written is consistent with God's will or self-will.

Next, the author instructs us to check what we have put on paper. Here is where your sponsor or sharing partner can be very helpful:

Check

"When in doubt and when it is important, what does another person who is living two-way prayer think about this thought or action? More light comes in through two windows than one. Someone else who also wants God's plan for our lives may help us see more clearly.

"Talk over together what you have written. Many people do this. They tell each other what guidance has come. This is the secret of unity. There are always three sides to every question—your side, my side, and the right side. Guidance shows us which is the right side—not who is right, but what is right."
("How to Listen to God," p. 3)

Then, the author explains what, to many of us, is the most difficult part of all:

Obey

"Carry out the thoughts that have come. You will only be sure of guidance as you go through with it. A rudder will not guide a boat until the boat is moving. As you obey, very often the results will convince you that you are on the right track."
("How to Listen to God," p. 3)

Remember, our Creator has given us free will. We're free **NOT** to listen to the God directed messages we receive. But, we must be prepared to accept the consequences if we choose not to follow God's plan for our lives.

If we don't receive any definite thoughts or ideas during our meditation, this is a sign we have additional work to do. There may still be **"things in ourselves which (have) been blocking us"**:

Blocks
". . . If I am not receiving thoughts when I listen, the fault is not God's.

"Usually it is because there is something *I will not do:*

- something wrong in my life that I will not face and make right;
- a habit or indulgence I will not give up;
- a person I will not forgive;
- a wrong relationship in my life I will not give up;
- a restitution I will not make;
- something God has already told me to do that I will not obey."

("How to Listen to God," pp. 3-4)

Look this list over. These items are described in the "Big Book" as part of the inventory and restitution process. If you have been thorough and honest in Steps Four through Nine, you will have removed the blocks that have prevented you from establishing and maintaining a two-way relationship with the God of your understanding.

So, you have two assignments for this week. Start making amends to those you've harmed and start practicing **"prayer and meditation"** on a daily basis. Write down your guidance and discuss it with your sponsor or sharing partner. Also bring it with you to the next meeting.

As for the results, they are summarized at the bottom of the fourth page of the "How to Listen to God" pamphlet:

> "There is a way of life, for everyone, everywhere. Anyone can be in touch with the living God, anywhere, anytime, *__if we fulfill His conditions:__*
>
> **When man listens, God speaks.**
> **When man obeys, God acts.**
>
> *__This is the law of prayer.__*"
> ("How to Listen to God," p. 4)

By making amends, you will convert the barriers that have separated you from others to bridges of reconciliation. By listening to the God of your understanding, you will be given the **"strength, inspiration and direction"** to change lives, starting with your own. Miracles are about to occur, and we look forward to hearing about them next session.

Are there any questions?

Chapter 5

Session #4–Steps 10, 11 and 12

This is our fourth journey back to the fall of 1946 and the A.A. Beginners' Meetings. During this session we will spend much of our time sharing the results of our two-way communication with the God of our understanding. We will experience the **"psychic change"** that occurs as we move from a **"life run on self-will"** to a life guided by **"the vision of God's will."**

We have demystified the Twelve Steps and shown you how simple this program truly is. For those who will be completing their Steps tonight, we congratulate you for your effort and we welcome you to the **"sunlight of the Spirit."**

Please remember that, in order to remain spiritually fit, we must be of service to other alcoholics. We can think of no greater service than helping newcomers through the Twelve Steps so they too can find the spiritual solution to their drinking problem.

It is important to remember that recovery is an ongoing process. We don't just take the Steps once and then **"rest on our laurels."** Keep in mind, **"alcohol is a subtle foe."** We must repeat the process again and again in order to **"keep in fit spiritual condition."**

So, please come back for the next series of Beginners' Meetings. We are sure you will gain additional insight into the "Big Book" and continue to enhance your relationship with the **"One who has all power."**

* *

WELCOME to the fourth of the one-hour A.A. Beginners' Meetings. This is the payoff. This is what we've been working for–to recover from the **"seemingly hopeless state of mind and body"** known as alcoholism. By taking the Twelve Steps, we experience the spiritual awakening that leads us to **"a new freedom and a new happiness."**

Our names are _____ and _____, and we are members of Alcoholics Anonymous. It is a pleasure to play a part in this life-changing process — to watch people grow spiritually right before our very eyes.

*(**Optional**) Are there any newcomers here tonight who do not have a sponsor or sharing partner with them right now? If so, please stand. We need to assign someone to help you during these sessions. [Ask for volunteers to assist those who are standing.] Thank you. Please be seated.*

Let's see who's ready to be rocketed into that **"fourth dimension of existence"** that the "Big Book" authors write about. Will those who have taken Steps One through Eight and are working on their Ninth Step amends, please stand.

Thank you. Please be seated. Some of you may not realize it yet, but you are in the process of experiencing the **"personality change sufficient to bring about recovery from alcoholism."**

We commend you for choosing to let the God of your understanding direct your lives. Now, it is time to expand upon this new God-consciousness. We do this by living Steps Ten, Eleven and Twelve on a daily basis.

The Tenth Step has us practice Steps Four through Nine on a regular basis. The Eleventh Step shows us how to improve our spiritual connection through prayer and meditation. The Twelfth Step provides us with guidelines for carrying our life-saving message to others. Let's start with the Tenth Step.

Step 10 *Continued to take personal inventory and when we were wrong promptly admitted it.*

In Steps One, Two and Three, we made the decisions that put us on the spiritual path. In Steps Four through Nine, we took the actions necessary to remove those things that have kept us separated from the God of our understanding. Now, we're ready to grow into the promised spiritual awakening.

The key to the Tenth Step is the word "continue." In the second paragraph on page 84, the "Big Book" authors emphasize the importance of continuing to take the Steps:

> "This . . . brings us to *Step Ten*, which suggests we continue to take personal inventory and continue to set right any new mistakes as we go along. We vigorously commenced this way of living as we cleaned up the past. We have entered the world of the Spirit. Our next function is to grow in understanding and effectiveness. This is not an overnight matter. It should continue for our lifetime."
> (*A.A.*, p. 84, para. 2, lines 1-8.)

125

In this paragraph, the authors explain how to live, one day at a time. We call this our twenty-four hour plan. We continue to take inventory, continue to make amends, and continue to help others every day.

Let's look at the third sentence in this paragraph again. It is very important. It reads, **"We have entered the world of the Spirit."**

This sentence contains an amazing revelation. Basically, the "Big Book" authors have just informed us that our lives have already been transformed as the result of taking Steps One through Nine. They state that we have had a **"revolutionary change in (our) way of living and thinking."**

How could that be? Well, it's very simple. There is no way a newcomer can take these Steps without **"divine help."** You have not only developed a belief in a God of your understanding, but you have come to rely upon this Power to guide you through the inventory and restitution process. You are now living in the solution.

On page 84, starting with the eighth line in the second paragraph, the authors summarize the process we use to remain spiritually connected:

> ". . . Continue to watch for selfishness, dishonesty, resentment, and fear. When these crop up, we ask God at once to remove them. We discuss them with someone immediately and make amends quickly if we have harmed anyone. Then we resolutely turn our thoughts to someone we can help.

Love and tolerance of others is our code."
(*A.A.*, p. 84, para. 2, lines 8-14)

In this paragraph, the "Big Book" authors present the A.A. test for self-will a second time. Two weeks ago, we described how to use this test to check the liabilities side of our Fourth Step inventory to determine if we needed to make amends. In the Tenth Step, the authors advise us to apply the same test, with minor variations, to our daily inventory. Here, they instruct us **"to watch for selfishness, dishonesty, resentment, and fear."**

The authors even provide us with specific directions on how to rid ourselves of these self-centered behaviors. First, we must realize they are not consistent with our Creator's plan for our lives. Next, we take the steps necessary to move from self-will to God's will. We discuss our shortcomings with our sponsor or sharing partner, ask the **"One who has all power"** to remove them, and, if necessary, **"set right the wrong(s)."** We then try to help someone else.

The "Big Book" authors state that if we follow this **"course of action"** on a daily basis, our obsession to drink will be removed. This is another of the many promises we find throughout the text of the book. In the third paragraph on page 84, they write:

> "And we have ceased fighting anything or anyone—
> even alcohol. For by this time sanity will have re-
> turned. We will seldom be interested in liquor. If
> tempted, we recoil from it as from a hot flame. We
> react sanely and normally, and we will find that this

has happened automatically. We will see that our new attitude toward liquor has been given us without any thought or effort on our part. It just comes! That is the miracle of it. We are not fighting it, neither are we avoiding temptation. We feel as though we had been placed in a position of neutrality—safe and protected. We have not even sworn off. Instead the problem has been removed. It does not exist for us. We are neither cocky nor are we afraid. That is our experience. That is how we react so long as we keep in fit spiritual condition."
(*A.A.*, p. 84, para. 3, lines 1-4; p. 85, lines 1-12)

How do we **"keep in fit spiritual condition?"** By taking a daily inventory. What is our reward? **"A daily reprieve."**

The "Big Book" authors describe this **"daily reprieve"** in the first paragraph on page 85:

"It is easy to let up on the spiritual program of action and rest on our laurels. We are headed for trouble if we do, for alcohol is a subtle foe. We are not cured of alcoholism. What we really have is a daily reprieve contingent on the maintenance of our spiritual condition. Every day is a day when we must carry the vision of God's will into all of our activities. 'How can I best serve Thee—Thy will (not mine) be done.' "
(*A.A.*, p. 85, para. 1, lines 1-8)

Another reward is God-consciousness — direct contact with the **"Spirit of the Universe."** In the second paragraph on page 85, the authors tell us:

"Much has already been said about receiving strength, inspiration, and direction from Him who has all knowledge and power. If we have carefully followed directions, we have begun to sense the flow of His Spirit into us. To some extent we have become God-conscious. We have begun to develop this vital sixth sense. But we must go further and that means more action."
(*A.A.*, p. 85, para. 2, lines 1-8)

Once again, they insist that our lives have already changed. We are now **"(conscious) of the Presence of God."** As we continue with the recovery process, the **"Power greater than ourselves"** will guide our thoughts and actions and strengthen our intuition–our **"vital sixth sense."**

Now it is time to find out who is ready to take the Tenth Step. The directions are in the second paragraph on page 84. Starting with the second line, the "Big Book" authors write:

"we continue to take personal inventory and continue to set right any new mistakes as we go along."
(*A.A.*, p. 84, para. 2, lines 2-3)

Will those who have taken the first Eight Steps and are working on their Ninth Step amends please stand. This is the Tenth Step question.

"Will you continue to take personal inventory and continue to set right any new mistakes as you go along?"

Please answer, one at a time, "yes" or "no." After you have answered, please be seated.

[Have each newcomer answer the question.]

Thank you.

According to the "Big Book" authors, those who answered "yes" to this question have taken Step Ten.

Now, let's move on to the Eleventh Step.

Step 11 *Sought through prayer and meditation to improve our conscious contact with God <u>as we understood Him,</u> praying only for knowledge of His will for us and the power to carry that out.*

This is the Step we prepared for last session. We are now going to examine **"prayer and meditation"** in more detail. Then, we will give everyone the opportunity to share the guidance they received while practicing the Eleventh Step during the past week.

The description of Step Eleven is found on pages 85 through 88. But, as we learned last week, the "Big Book" authors have been writing about two-way prayer throughout the book.

In the third paragraph on page 85, the authors advise us to conduct an Eleventh Step on a regular basis:

> "*Step Eleven* suggests prayer and meditation. We shouldn't be shy on this matter of prayer. Better men

than we are using it constantly. It works, if we have
the proper attitude and work at it."
(*A.A.*, p. 85, para. 3, lines 1-2; p. 86, lines 1-2)

"Prayer and meditation" puts us directly in contact with
the **"Power greater than ourselves."** Hopefully, that's what
each of us has been doing this past week — praying and listening to the source of **"all knowledge and power."**

Starting with the second line on page 86, they make this
statement:

". . .It would be easy
to be vague about this matter. Yet, we believe we can
make some definite and valuable suggestions."
(*A.A.*, p. 86, lines 2-4)

Then, the "Big Book" authors provide step-by-step instructions on how to practice two-way prayer. They explain what
we are to do at night, in the morning, and throughout the day.

At night, we review the day's activities. In the first paragraph on page 86, the authors write:

"When we retire at night, we constructively review
our day. Were we resentful, selfish, dishonest or
afraid? Do we owe an apology? Have we kept something to ourselves which should be discussed with
another person at once? Were we kind and loving
toward all? What could we have done better? Were
we thinking of ourselves most of the time? Or were
we thinking of what we could do for others, of

what we could pack into the stream of life?"
(*A.A.*, p. 86, para. 1, lines 1-9)

This paragraph contains the third reference to the A.A. test for self-will. The "Big Book" authors once again have made minor changes to the test they presented to us in the Fourth and Tenth Steps. Nevertheless, it is still the opposite of the test for God's will based on the Four Standards:

Test for self-will	Test for God's will
Resentful	**Purity**
Selfish(ness)	**Unselfishness**
Dishonest(y)	**Honesty**
Afraid (or Fear)	**Love**

We use this same test during our morning meditation to check our guidance.

In the second paragraph on page 86, the authors provide us with directions for conducting a daily "quiet time":

"On awakening let us think about the twenty-four hours ahead. We consider our plans for the day. Before we begin, we ask God to direct our thinking, especially asking that it be divorced from self-pity, dishonest or self-seeking motives."
(*A.A.*, p. 86, para. 2, lines 1-5)

Let's look at the third sentence again. It reads, "**Before we begin, we ask God to direct our thinking, . . .**" Please concentrate on these words. They are very important. "**Before we begin,**" — before we begin what? Before we begin listening to

God. How do we know we're supposed to listen to God? Because immediately afterward it says, **"we ask God to direct our thinking."** If we ask God to direct our thinking, doesn't it stand to reason that our next thoughts and ideas are going to come from God? What do we do with these thoughts and ideas? We write them down. Why? So we won't forget them.

After putting our guidance on paper, we check it against the A.A. test for self-will. We do this because not everything we receive during our period of meditation comes from God. However, with time and practice we will begin to trust **"our vital sixth sense."** Starting with the first sentence on page 87, the "Big Book" authors explain:

> "What used to be the hunch or the occasional inspiration gradually becomes a working part of the mind. Being still inexperienced and having just made conscious contact with God, it is not probable that we are going to be inspired at all times. We might pay for this presumption in all sorts of absurd actions and ideas. Nevertheless, we find that our thinking will, as time passes, be more and more on the plane of inspiration. We come to rely upon it."
> (*A.A.*, p. 87, lines 1-9)

In December 1934, Bill W., our New York City cofounder, used the Four Standards of Honesty, Purity, Unselfishness and Love to check his guidance. In the fourth paragraph on page 13, Bill states:

> "I was to test my thinking by the new God-consciousness within. Common sense would thus become un-

common sense."
(*A.A.*, p. 13, para. 4, lines 1-3)

For Bill, it was **"common sense"** to use alcohol to escape his problems, and **"uncommon sense"** to stay sober and let God guide him through his difficulties. Bill's life changed as the direct result of listening to and following guidance.

In 1939, the "Big Book" authors gave us the opposites of the Four Standards as a way to check what we think, say and do. As for our daily meditation, here's how it works. When we finish our "quiet time," we check what we have put on paper. If what we have written is Honest, Pure, Unselfish **AND** Loving, we can be assured these thoughts or ideas are consistent with God's will. Conversely, if what we have written is Dishonest, Resentful, Selfish **OR** Fearful, we can be equally assured these thoughts or ideas are consistent with self-will.

The authors indicate it is during our "quiet time" that our questions will be answered. In the third paragraph on page 86, they reveal how the One **"who has all knowledge and power"** is going to respond to our requests for help:

> "In thinking about our day we may face indecision. We may not be able to determine which course to take. Here we ask God for inspiration, an intuitive thought or a decision. We relax and take it easy. We don't struggle. We are often surprised how the right answers come after we have tried this for a while."
> (*A.A.*, p. 86, para. 3, lines 1-6)

So, according to the "Big Book" authors, God is going to communicate with us through **"inspiration, an intuitive thought, or a decision."** If the **"inner resource"** is going to supply us with **"the right answers,"** wouldn't it be a good idea to jot them down so we can review them from time to time?

We close our time of **"prayer and meditation"** by asking God to guide us throughout our daily activities. In the first paragraph on page 87, the "Big Book" authors write:

> "We usually conclude the period of meditation with a prayer that we be shown all through the day what our next step is to be, that we be given whatever we need to take care of such problems. We ask especially for freedom from self-will, and are careful to make no request for ourselves only."
> (*A.A.*, p. 87, para. 1, lines 1-6)

The authors then describe what we are to do anytime we become troubled or confused. We relax and ask for guidance. Starting with the third paragraph on page 87, they suggest that:

> "As we go through the day we pause, when agitated or doubtful, and ask for the right thought or action. We constantly remind ourselves we are no longer running the show, humbly saying to ourselves many times each day 'Thy will be done.' We are then in much less danger of excitement, fear, anger, worry, self-pity, or foolish decisions. We become much more efficient. We do not tire so easily, for we are not burning up energy foolishly as we did when we were trying to arrange life to suit ourselves.
>
> "It works—it really does."

(*A.A.*, p. 87, para. 3 lines 1-3; p. 88, lines 1-7; para.1, line 1)

This is an ironclad guarantee. **"It works!"** From first-hand experience, we can state that two-way prayer has been working in our lives ever since we began a daily "quiet time."

But, what if we don't receive any God given thoughts or ideas? Let us assure you, this can happen at any time. Remember, all **"we really have is a daily reprieve contingent upon the maintenance of our spiritual condition."** If we don't feel **"the Presence of God,"** it means we have work to do. Maybe we've taken back our will in some area of our lives, or, maybe we haven't made a necessary amends. If this is the case, we take the actions that reconnect us to the source of **"all knowledge and power."**

Starting with the second paragraph on page 88, the "Big Book" authors state, once again, that we need God's help:

> "We alcoholics are undisciplined. So we let God
> discipline us in the simple way we have just outlined.
> "But this is not all. There is action and more action.
> 'Faith without works is dead.' "
> (*A.A.*, p. 88, para. 2, lines 1-2; para. 3, lines 1-2)

In order for two-way prayer to be effective, we must constantly practice being in the presence of God. If we do the work, we will receive the rewards — a life filled with **"power, peace, happiness, and . . . direction."**

We will conclude our presentation of the Eleventh Step

with a moment of silence so each of us can make contact with the **"Spirit of the Universe"** and receive guidance right now. Please write down any thoughts or ideas you receive during this "quiet time."

[Observe two to three minutes of silence.]

Thank you. At the end of the last session, we asked you to meditate during the week and write down the guidance that came to you. We realize these thoughts and ideas can be very personal and are normally discussed with your sponsor or sharing partner. However, if you believe what you have written passes the test for God's will and can be of benefit to others, we ask that you share it now with the group. In addition, you will be helping those who are still struggling with the Eleventh Step to see how **"God will constantly disclose more to you and to us."**

Who's willing to share what they have written either during the past week or during tonight's "quiet time?"

[For the next 10-15 minutes, have those who are practicing two-way prayer share their **WRITTEN** guidance.]

Thank you. Whether you shared guidance or listened to others share their guidance, you have taken Step Eleven. We can now proceed to the Twelfth Step.

Step 12 *Having had a spiritual awakening as the result of these steps, we tried to carry this message to alcoholics, and to practice these principles in all*

___

our affairs.

Now that we've made conscious contact with the God of our understanding, we have received the greatest gift of this program — a spiritual awakening. God is now guiding us **"in a way which is indeed miraculous."**

This life-changing experience comes suddenly to some, gradually to others. In Appendix II on page 567, we learn more about this amazing **"transformation of thought and attitude."**

This appendix was written after the publication of the first printing of the "Big Book" in 1939. In the first printing, the Twelfth Step read:

"Having had a spiritual experience as the result of these steps, . . ."

During the two years between the first and second printings, the word **"experience"** was discussed at length. Eventually, **"experience"** was replaced with the word **"awakening."** The "Big Book" authors made this modification in order to include those whose lives had truly changed, but more slowly over a period of time.

Many of you will find this to be the case also. Your life has changed, but gradually rather than suddenly. You may not be able to point to a specific experience that brought about the change, but the spiritual awakening has occurred nonetheless.

Starting with the first line on page 567, the authors define **"spiritual experience"** and **"spiritual awakening"**:

"The terms 'spiritual experience' and 'spiritual awakening' are used many times in this book which, upon careful reading, shows that the personality change sufficient to bring about recovery from alcoholism has manifested itself among us in many different forms.

"Yet it is true that our first printing gave many readers the impression that these personality changes, or religious experiences, must be in the nature of sudden and spectacular upheavals. Happily for everyone, this conclusion is erroneous."
(*A.A.*, p. 567, para. 1, lines 1-5; para.2, lines 1-5)

A spiritual awakening is nothing more than a **"psychic change"** that, among other things, removes our obsession to drink. So, Bill W.'s rapid conversion experience in Towns Hospital is an exception rather than the rule.

In the fourth paragraph on page 567, the authors describe a more gradual spiritual experience:

"Among our rapidly growing membership of thousands of alcoholics such transformations, though frequent, are by no means the rule. Most of our experiences are what the psychologist William James calls the 'educational variety' because they develop slowly over a period of time. Quite often friends of the newcomer are aware of the difference long before he is himself. He finally realizes that he has undergone a profound alteration in his reaction to life; that such a change could hardly have been brought about by himself alone. What often takes place in a few months could seldom have been accomplished by years of self-discipline. With few exceptions our members find that they have tapped an unsuspected inner resource which they presently identify with their

own conception of a Power greater than themselves."
(*A.A.*, p. 567, para. 4, lines 1-13; p. 568, lines 1-2)

Let's look at the fifth sentence again. It reads, **"What often takes place in a few months could seldom have been accomplished by years of self discipline."** The "Big Book" authors make it clear that, if you take the Steps and then help others through them, you will recover within **"a few months."**

We realize that some will have a conversion experience during the first month, but others may not "get it" right away. Nevertheless, you will still have a gradual spiritual awakening as the result of going through the process again and again.

This is one of the greatest promises in the "Big Book." Just think of it. Even under the most difficult circumstances, if you do the work you will overcome your drinking problem in about ninety days or so.

In the first paragraph on page 568, we learn how easy it is to have the promised spiritual awakening:

> "Most of us think this awareness of a Power greater than ourselves is the essence of spiritual experience. Our more religious members call it 'God-consciousness.' "
> (*A.A.*, p. 568, para. 1, lines 1-3)

That's all there is to it. If you've made conscious contact with the God of your understanding and you have started listening to guidance, you have, in fact, had the **"psychic change."** You are now living in the **"sunlight of the Spirit."**

Now, let's look at what we have to do in order to maintain

this spiritual transformation. Chapter 7, in its entirety, is devoted to carrying the message of Alcoholics Anonymous to others. In the first paragraph on page 89, the "Big Book" authors tell us how to expand our new God-consciousness:

*P*RACTICAL EXPERIENCE shows that nothing will so much insure immunity from drinking as intensive work with other alcoholics. It works when other activities fail. This is our *twelfth suggestion:* Carry this message to other alcoholics! You can help when no one else can. You can secure their confidence when others fail."
(A.A., p. 89, para. 1, lines 1-7)

When **WE** work with others, **OUR** lives change. In the second paragraph on page 89, the authors state:

"Life will take on new meaning. To watch people recover, to see them help others, to watch loneliness vanish, to see a fellowship grow up about you, to have a host of friends—this is an experience you must not miss. We know you will not want to miss it. Frequent contact with newcomers and with each other is the bright spot of our lives."
(*A.A.*, p. 89, para. 2, lines 1-7)

On pages 89 through 103, the "Big Book" authors provide us with specific instructions on how to carry our lifesaving message of recovery to others. They offer many valuable suggestions on these pages. Here are a few of them.

In the first paragraph on page 90, they offer this advice:

"When you discover a prospect for Alcoholics Anonymous, find out all you can about him. If he does not want to stop drinking, don't waste time trying to persuade him. You may spoil a later opportunity."
(*A.A.*, p. 90, para. 1, lines 1-4)

In the third paragraph on page 91, the authors give us specific directions on what to say. We begin by telling **"our story"**:

"See your man alone, if possible. At first engage in general conversation. After a while, turn the talk to some phase of drinking. Tell him enough about your drinking habits, symptoms, and experiences to encourage him to speak of himself. If he wishes to talk, let him do so. You will thus get a better idea of how you ought to proceed."
(*A.A.*, p. 91, para. 3, lines 1-7)

Then we explain how we recovered. In the first paragraph on page 94, the "Big Book" authors write:

"Outline the program of action, explaining how you made a self-appraisal, how you straightened out your past and why you are now endeavoring to be helpful to him. It is important for him to realize that your attempt to pass this on to him plays a vital part in your own recovery."
(*A.A.*, p. 94, para. 1, lines 1-6)

On page 95, starting with the tenth line in the first paragraph, the authors ask us to treat the prospect with dignity and respect:

> "Never talk down to an alcoholic from any moral or spiritual hilltop; simply lay out the kit of spiritual tools for his inspection. Show him how they worked with you. Offer him friendship and fellowship. Tell him that if he wants to get well you will do anything to help."
> (*A.A.*, p. 95, para. 1, lines 10-15)

Even if we are unsuccessful in getting through to the prospect, the authors encourage us not to give up. In the first paragraph on page 96, they advise us to plant the seed and move on:

> "Do not be discouraged if your prospect does not respond at once. Search out another alcoholic and try again. You are sure to find someone desperate enough to accept with eagerness what you offer. We find it a waste of time to keep chasing a man who cannot or will not work with you. If you leave such a person alone, he may soon become convinced that he cannot recover by himself. To spend too much time on any one situation is to deny some other alcoholic an opportunity to live and be happy."
> (*A.A.*, p. 96, para. 1, lines 1-10)

On page 98, starting with the fifth line in the first paragraph, they tell us what to do about the person who makes one excuse after another as to why he or she can't stop drinking:

> ". . . He clamors for this or that, claiming he cannot master

alcohol until his material needs are cared for. Non-sense. Some of us have taken very hard knocks to learn this truth: Job or no job—wife or no wife—we simply do not stop drinking so long as we place dependence upon other people ahead of dependence on God.

"Burn the idea into the consciousness of every man that he can get well regardless of anyone. The only condition is that he trust in God and clean house." (*A.A.*, p. 98, para. 1, lines 5-12; para. 2, lines 1-3)

How much simpler can it get? **"Trust in God and clean house."**

In the first paragraph on page 100, the "Big Book" authors inform us that we grow spiritually when we work with new-comers:

"Both you and the new man must walk day by day in the path of spiritual progress. If you persist, remarkable things will happen. When we look back, we realize that the things which came to us when we put ourselves in God's hands were better than anything we could have planned. Follow the dictates of a Higher Power and you will presently live in a new and wonderful world, no matter what your present circumstances!" (*A.A.*, p. 100, para. 1, lines 1-9)

Back on page 63, the authors stated that God is our **"new Employer."** Now, in the second paragraph on page 102, they provide us with a new job description:

"Your job now is to be at the place where you may be of maximum helpfulness to others, so never hesitate to go anywhere if you can be helpful. You should not hesitate to visit the most sordid spot on earth on such an errand. Keep on the firing line of life with these motives and God will keep you unharmed."
(*A.A.*, p. 102, para. 2, lines 1-6)

This concludes our presentation of Step Twelve as found in our "Big Book." Let God guide you when you make your Twelfth Step calls and the **"Spirit of the Universe"** will keep you safe and protected. In addition, by relying upon guidance, you **WILL "be of maximum service to God and the people about (you)."**

Being of service to others is critical to our continued growth and the maintenance of our sobriety. Keep in mind that one of the primary services we can perform is to take newcomers through the Twelve Steps. Each time we do this, we learn more about our lifesaving program and gain additional insight into the **"All Powerful Creator"** who is at the heart of our new way of living.

Who knows, maybe in a couple of months, some of you will be ready to lead these sessions. As we have discovered, conducting these Beginners' Meetings is a real test of how well **WE** know the "Big Book."

Now, all that's left is to practice these principles on a daily basis. What principles? The Twelve Steps of Alcoholics Anonymous! These are the principles we rely upon in order to remain in the **"sunlight of the Spirit"** for the rest of our lives.

It is time to make a commitment to work with others. Will those who have taken the first Eleven Steps, please stand. This is the Twelfth Step question.

"Will you carry this message to other alcoholics?"

Please answer, one at a time, "yes" or "no." After you have answered, please be seated.

[Have each newcomer answer the question.]

According to the "Big Book" authors, those who answered "yes" to this question have taken Step Twelve. This is a monumental achievement. Congratulations.

We are going to close this session by reading two key passages about the recovery process. The first one is on page 164, starting with the second paragraph. It emphasizes the importance of guidance and the necessity of working with others:

> "Our book is meant to be suggestive only. We realize we know only a little. God will constantly disclose more to you and to us. Ask Him in your morning meditation what you can do each day for the man who is still sick. The answers will come, if your own house is in order. But obviously you cannot transmit something you haven't got. See to it that your relationship with Him is right, and great events will come to pass for you and countless others. This is the Great Fact for us.
>
> "Abandon yourself to God as you understand God. Admit your faults to Him and to your fellows. Clear

away the wreckage of your past. Give freely of what you find and join us. We shall be with you in the Fellowship of the Spirit, and you will surely meet some of us as you trudge the Road of Happy Destiny.

"May God bless you and keep you—until then." (*A.A.*, p. 164, para. 2, lines 1-10; para. 3, lines 1-6; para. 4, line 1)

The second passage is on page 25. We have waited until now to share the first two paragraphs of this page with you because, when we started this journey, you might not have understood the significance of what is written here. Having taken the Twelve Steps and having had a spiritual awakening, you are now in a position to see these words from an entirely new perspective. Your life has changed. You now realize, ***"There is a Solution."***

". . . Almost none of us liked the self-searching, the leveling of our pride, the confession of shortcomings which the process requires for its successful consummation. But we saw that it really worked in others, and we had come to believe in the hopelessness and futility of life as we had been living it. When, therefore, we were approached by those in whom the problem had been solved, there was nothing left for us but to pick up the simple kit of spiritual tools laid at our feet. We have found much of heaven and we have been rocketed into a fourth dimension of existence of which we had not even dreamed.

"The great fact is just this, and nothing less: That we have had deep and effective spiritual experiences which have revolutionized our whole attitude toward life, toward our fellows and toward God's universe. The central fact of our lives today is the absolute certainty that our Creator has entered into our hearts and lives in a way which is indeed miraculous. He has commenced to accomplish those things for us which we could never do by ourselves."

(*A.A.*, p. 25, para. 1, lines 1-12; para. 2, lines 1-9)

We wish to welcome those who have taken all Twelve Steps to the **"fourth dimension of existence."** We thank you for the opportunity to be your guides for this miraculous spiritual journey.

Are there any questions?

(*Optional*) [*After all questions have been answered, the meeting leader brings the session to an end.*]

Please remain seated. We will close this meeting with a moment of silence followed by the Lord's Prayer.

Chapter 6

Summary

I am truly blessed to have had a spiritual guide who, not only attended the Beginners' Meetings in the mid-1950's, but conducted workshops based on this "original" A.A. format for the better part of forty years. He provided me with a great deal of insight into how the Beginners' Meetings worked and why they were so successful. In addition he critiqued my early attempts to recreate the four one-hour sessions.

I started leading Beginners' Meetings in 1995 after my spiritual guide challenged me to stop talking about the sessions and start doing something about them. "Two years of research is enough," he said. "You need to take some action."

He told me, "You have to get out of flight school. Take what you've learned and put it to the test. It's time to fly the plane."

This was a terrifying proposition for someone who, prior to A.A., had a deep-seated fear of speaking in public. But, I walked through the fear and prayed for guidance each step of the way. As I saw people recover from alcoholism right before my eyes, I grew more and more confident that God was leading me **"in a way which (was) indeed miraculous."**

After completing my first "solo flight" of Beginners' Meetings, I realized my spiritual guide had been quite astute when he told me, "The only way to understand the 'Big Book' is to try to explain it to someone else." In the ensuing years I've discovered there is always more to be learned about this remarkable textbook for recovery.

In addition to the "gentle push" I received from my spiritual guide to revive the Beginners' Meetings, I was also motivated by an incident that occurred in 1993. At that time, I was just beginning to collect material on the four one-hour sessions.

I was speaking on the history of Alcoholics Anonymous at a Saturday night meeting in Scottsdale, Arizona. During my presentation, I mentioned Earl T., an A.A. pioneer from Chicago, Illinois. His story in the "Big Book" is titled, "He Sold Himself Short." In his autobiography, Earl explains how he took the Steps with Dr. Bob in one afternoon.

In February 1938, Earl traveled from Chicago, Illinois to Akron, Ohio to get help for his alcoholism. After being "indoctrinated" by eight or nine individuals, Earl attended his first meeting.

The fellowship of Alcoholics Anonymous did not exist at the time. It evolved after the publication of the "Big Book" in April 1939. But, Bill W. had already taken the Oxford Group's "Four Spiritual Activities" and modified them for the Akron "alcoholic squadron" and the New York "nameless bunch of drunks."

This is how Earl T. took the Steps:

> "The day before I was due to go back to Chicago—
> it was Dr. Bob's afternoon off—he had me to the
> office and we spent three or four hours formally
> going through the Six-Step program as it was at that

time. The six steps were:

1. Complete deflation. [A.A.'s Steps 1, 2 and 3]
2. Dependence and guidance from a Higher Power. [A.A.'s Step 11]
3. Moral inventory. [A.A.'s Steps 4 and 10]
4. Confession. [A.A.'s Steps 5, 6 and 7]
5. Restitution. [A.A.'s Steps 8 and 9]
6. Continued work with other alcoholics. [A.A.'s Step 12]

"Dr. Bob led me through all of these steps. At the moral inventory, he brought up several of my bad personality traits or character defects, such as selfishness, conceit, jealousy, carelessness, intolerance, ill-temper, sarcasm and resentments. We went over these at great length, and then he finally asked me if I wanted these defects of character removed. When I said yes, we both knelt at his desk and prayed, each of us asking to have these defects taken away."
(*A.A.*, p. 262, para. 6, line 1; p. 263, lines 1-10; para. 1, lines 1-9)

In a couple of hours, Dr. Bob and Earl put together and discussed Earl's list of character liabilities. This is the second reference in the "Big Book" to a newcomer taking the equivalent of the Fourth and Fifth Steps in one sitting. The first one is Bill W., whom Ebby T. took through the Four Spiritual Activities of Surrender (A.A.'s Steps 1, 2 and 3), Sharing (A.A.'s Steps 4, 5, 6 and 7), Restitution (A.A.'s Steps 8 and 9), and Guidance (A.A.'s Steps 10, 11 and 12) in one day. [See pages 13-14 of "Bill's Story."]

Dr. Bob used an assets and liabilities checklist to take Earl

151

through the moral inventory. This format was used throughout the A.A. fellowship during the 1940's and 1950's. In 1938, Dr. Bob's checklist contained eight liabilities. They were: **SELFISH-NESS, CONCEIT, JEALOUSY, CARELESSNESS, INTOL-ERANCE, ILL-TEMPER, SARCASM** and **RESENTMENT.**

During this Saturday night meeting in Scottsdale, I also brought up Clarence S., another A.A. pioneer. His story in the Third Edition of the "Big Book" is titled, "Home Brewmeister."

In February 1938, Dr. Bob took Clarence through the Steps, and Clarence found a spiritual solution for his alcoholism. Later, Clarence played an instrumental role in the explosive growth of A.A. in the Cleveland, Ohio area during the early 1940's.

Clarence would take newcomers through the Steps in a weekend. He called the process "fixing rummies." He'd say, "Come to me on Friday evening on Step One and by the time you leave on Sunday morning you'll have taken all Twelve Steps. Then, in order to stay 'fixed,' you'll need to practice Steps Ten, Eleven and Twelve on a daily basis."

Clarence also used an assets and liabilities checklist to take newcomers through the Steps. He relied upon the seventeen-item Moral Inventory published in the June 1946 issue of *The A.A. Grapevine.*

At the conclusion of the Saturday evening meeting in Scottsdale, a man came up to me and said, "Wally, I am confused. I just paid $18,000 for 21 days of treatment and I am now in aftercare. I go to individual therapy, group therapy and A.A.

meetings. Both my therapist and my A.A. sponsor told me to take one Step a year."

"I thought it a bit far-fetched that it would take twelve years to complete the Steps, but I didn't question what these people told me. Tonight, you talked about taking the Steps in a couple of hours. Now, I don't know what to think."

I was shocked to learn that some people within the recovery community had placed such a formidable barrier between the newcomer and the solution to his or her problem. Before this conversation, I had never heard anyone say, "Take one Step a year."

I replied, "I can't speak for you, but I do know that if anyone had told me to take one Step a year, I'd have been drunk before I ever got to the Second Step. The question you need to ask is, 'Where in the text of the 'Big Book' does it say to take one Step a year?' It's not in there. As far as I am concerned, if what you hear isn't in the 'Big Book,' it's not part of the A.A. program."

I wish this conversation had turned out to be an isolated incident, but I'm sorry to say this has not been the case. I've heard this "one Step a year" philosophy along with "no Steps for the first year" espoused many times since 1993.

I am so fortunate to have been told right from the beginning of my spiritual journey that, "The program is contained in one book and one book only–the 'Big Book' of *Alcoholics Anonymous*. The 'Twelve and Twelve' and other books can provide additional information, but they don't contain the instructions on how to take the Steps. Stick with the 'Big Book' — read it every day."

Over the years, I've seen many well-intentioned people add layer upon layer of complexity to the "Big Book" directions. I've talked to people who have left treatment centers with "all the answers." They "graduate" with notebooks containing hundreds of pages of material on alcoholism and mini-novels on their first three Steps.

In order to get back to the "original" program of recovery, we must first know what the "original" program was. In the early days, "Keep it simple" was more than just a slogan–it was a way of life. How the old-timers actually practiced the A.A. program during the highly successful early days of the fellowship is quite different from how most A.A.'s today think they practiced it.

In the course of conducting research for this book, I talked with many A.A. old-timers who provided me with information that was quite surprising and, in some cases, almost unimaginable compared to the current A.A. program. I tried to keep an open mind about what they told me, especially since they had experienced such positive results. A few of their more enlightening revelations follow:

1. *Most early A.A.'s never did a written Fourth Step.* I interviewed more than one hundred A.A. pioneers from the 1940's and early 1950's. Only a few of them put anything on paper in terms of an inventory. Whether they wrote anything or not, they did work together with their sponsors or sharing partners.

So, what about the three-column inventory described on page 65 of the "Big Book?" Isn't that the inventory we're supposed to use as our guide because "it's in the book?" All I can say is that, even though Bill W. took it upon himself to include it in the "Big Book," neither he nor any other A.A. pioneer from the 1940's used this inventory to take the Steps or to take anyone else through them. Of the old-timers I interviewed, every one of them who did a written Fourth Step used the "commercial inventory" described on page 64.

2. *The role of the sponsor in early A.A. was limited.* Many old-timers reported that the group as a whole sponsored them rather than any particular individual.

   In the areas of North America where the Beginners' Meetings were held, the sponsor or sharing partner's commitment to the newcomer was usually four to five weeks. After the newcomer completed the four one-hour sessions, both the sponsor or sharing partner and the newcomer moved on to help others through the Steps.

3. *The sponsor's responsibilities were clearly defined.* Two pamphlets on sponsorship were distributed during the mid-1940's. The Cleveland Central Committee published the first one, *A • A Sponsorship–Its Opportunities and Responsibilities,* in 1944. In the pamphlet the authors make the following statements:

   "Any A.A. who has not experienced the joys and satisfaction of helping another alcoholic regain his place in life has not yet fully realized the complete benefits of this fellowship.

155

"To give the new member a broad and complete picture of A.A., the sponsor should take him to various meetings within convenient distance of his home. Attending several meetings gives the new man a chance to select a group in which he will be most happy and comfortable . . . .

"These suggestions for sponsoring a new man in A.A. . . . are by no means complete. They are intended only as a framework and general guide. Each individual case is different and should be treated as such." [30]

The second pamphlet on sponsorship, *A Manual for Alcoholics Anonymous*, was authorized by A.A.'s cofounder, Dr. Bob, and published by the Akron, Ohio Group sometime prior to 1946. It contains sections titled, "To the Newcomer" and "To the Sponsor."

In the section "To the Sponsor," the author wrote:

"You must assume full responsibility for this man. You must fulfill all pledges you make to him, either tangible or intangible. If you cannot fulfill a promise, do not make it.

"This is a very critical time in his life. He looks to you for courage, hope, comfort and guidance. He fears the past. He is uncertain of the future. And he is in a frame of mind that the least neglect on your

---

30 Anonymous, *A•A Sponsorship–Its Opportunities and Its Responsibilities* (Cleveland, OH: Cleveland Ohio District Office, 1944) 3,5,10,11.

part will fill him with resentment and self-pity. You have in your hands the most valuable property in the world—the future of a fellow man. Treat his life as carefully as you would your own. You are literally responsible for his life.

"Accompany him to his first meeting. Take him along with you when you call on the next patient. Telephone him when there are other patients. Drop in at his home occasionally. Telephone him as often as possible. Urge him to look up the new friends he has made." [31]

The author of the Akron pamphlet states that it is the responsibility of the sponsor to call the newcomer. This seems rather obvious, considering it is the newcomer who is sick and needs help. Somehow, this concept has been lost to many A.A.'s today.

4. *In most areas, the Beginners' Meetings were sponsored and funded by an A.A. Home Group.* Consequently, the basket was not passed during the four one-hour sessions.

In Miami, Florida and Boston, Massachusetts, the local Intergroup Office funded the Beginners' Meetings because they were considered to be Twelfth Step service work. When an A.A. answered a call for help, he or she would talk to the prospect, if necessary get the prospect into a hospital, and then accompany the prospect to the Beginners' Meetings. The Twelfth Step call was not considered to be complete until the A.A. took the newcomer through the Steps.

---

31 Anonymous (Evan W.), *A Manual for Alcoholics Anonymous* (Akron, OH: A.A. of Akron, Undated) 3,4.

5. *Although the Beginners' Meetings were a significant part of the recovery process, they were only designed to give the newcomer a rough overview of the A.A. program.* The Beginners' Meetings were not a substitute for, but rather a supplement to the Open Speaker and Closed Discussion meet ings that were also part of the "original" A.A. program.

The authors of the Washington, DC pamphlet made this clear when they wrote:

> "The material contained herein is merely an outline of the . . . program and is not intended to replace or supplant—
>
> a) The careful reading and re-reading of the "Big Book."
> b) Regular attendance at **weekly** group meetings.
> c) Study of the Program.
> d) Daily practice of the Program.
> e) Reading of approved printed matter on Alcoholism [approved by the Group].
> f) Informal discussions with other members.
>
> "This instruction is not a short-cut to A.A. It is an introduction—a brief course in the fundamentals." [32]

A.A.'s cofounder, Dr. Bob, is well known for his commitment to **"working with others."** From 1939 until his death in 1950, he treated alcoholics at St. Thomas Hospital in Akron, Ohio. During these eleven years, he took approximately 5,000

---

32 Anonymous, *Alcoholics Anonymous–An Interpretation of Our Twelve Steps* (Washington, D.C.: Paragon Creative Printers, September, 1944) 9.

alcoholics through the Steps, which is more than *one person per day*. He was so successful, Bill W. called him the "Prince of the Twelve Steppers."

Just as he had done with Earl T., Dr. Bob took each newcomer through the Steps quickly. Duke P. (sobriety date: August 15, 1940) tells how Dr. Bob took him through the Fourth and Fifth Steps in about an hour. During that time, Dr. Bob had Duke look at his assets as well as his liabilities. Dr. Bob told him to, "Keep it simple, and lubricate it with love." [33]

The assets and liabilities checklist that Dr. Bob and many of the A.A. pioneers used for the moral inventory came directly from the Oxford Group. In *What Is the Oxford Group?*, which was written anonymously in 1933, the author describes the process that later became A.A.'s Fourth and Fifth Steps:

> "Sharing of faults as practiced by the Group is sharing in the ordinary sense of the word. In plain language it is telling, or talking over, our shortcomings with another who has already surrendered his or her life to God." [34]

In 1934, Victor Kitchen, one of the many recovered alcoholics in the Oxford Group, wrote *I was a Pagan*. Victor attended meetings at the Calvary Church in New York City with

---

33 Audio taped interview of Duke P. conducted by Wally P. on December 4, 1994.

34 The Layman with a Notebook, *What Is the Oxford Group?* (London: Oxford University Press, 1933) 27

Bill W. for several years. In the book, Victor described his assets and liabilities checklist:

> "I felt that my character possessed many negative attributes such as fear, anger, revenge and false pride; and that it also held many positive potentialities such as poise, good nature, sympathy and understanding. I tried to make a chart of these things, showing which qualities fell on the positive side and which on the negative." [35]

In *When Man Listens,* Cecil Rose described the "commercial inventory" that the "Big Book" authors refer to on page 64:

> "If a man is bankrupt and consents to a reorganization of the business, the first thing he must do is produce the books—all of them. The difficulty with so many debtors is that they conceal some of the debts, or fail to mention some particularly foolish blunder or some doubtful transaction. A satisfactory reorganization is impossible if there is only a partial disclosure. If we want God to take control of our lives, the first thing we must do is to produce the books. We must be willing to look, with God, at everything." [36]

Cecil used the Four Standards for the assets side of the ledger:

---

35 Victor Kitchen, *I Was a Pagan* (New York, NY: Harper & Brothers, 1934) 6

36 Cecil Rose, *When Man Listens* (New York, NY: Oxford University Press, 1937) 17

> "A good way to begin this examination of the books is to test our lives beside the Sermon on the Mount. A convenient and pointed summary of its teaching has been made under the four headings of Honesty, Purity, Unselfishness and Love." [37]

Several Oxford Group authors described the liabilities side of the ledger in great detail. A. J. Russell, the author of *For Sinners Only*, listed liabilities under four general headings. These were Dishonesty, Impurity, Selfishness and Fear, which were essentially the same attributes the "Big Book" authors used as a test for self-will in A.A.'s Fourth, Tenth and Eleventh Steps.

In the early days of A.A., various checklists were used to take newcomers through the inventory and restitution process. Dr. Bob used eight assets and liabilities, the Washington, DC pamphlet contained six, the June 1946 issue of *The A.A. Grapevine* listed seventeen, and the *Twelve Steps and Twelve Traditions*, published in 1952, also had eight.

In the January 1952 issue of *The A.A. Grapevine*, the editorial board published an article on the Fourth Step Inventory:

> "One practical way of starting this very practical Step is to prepare a record sheet with two columns, one headed, 'Liabilities' and the other, 'Assets.' " [38]

---

37 Cecil Rose, *When Man Listens* (New York, NY: Oxford University Press, 1937) 18

38 Anonymous (Editorial Staff), *The A.A. Grapevine* (New York, NY: The Alcoholic Foundation, 1952) 2

In the "Twelve and Twelve," the Fourth Step is described in considerable detail as an assets and liabilities checklist. There is no mention whatsoever of the "three-column inventory" found on page 65 of the "Big Book,"

How can this be? Well, it's very simple. The "three-column inventory" was not mentioned because it was not used to take newcomers through the Fourth Step at the time the "Twelve and Twelve" was written:

> ". . . Nearly every serious emotional problem can be seen as a case of misdirected instinct. When that happens, our great natural **ASSETS**, the instincts, have turned into physical and mental **LIABILITIES.**
>
> "Step Four is our vigorous and painstaking effort to discover what these **LIABILITIES** in each of us have been, and are."
> (*Twelve Steps and Twelve Traditions*, p. 42)

On page 48, the author stated that there were several assets and liabilities checklists in use. Then he described a list based on the Seven Deadly Sins.

> "To avoid falling into confusion over the names these defects should be called, let's take a universally recognized list of major human failings–the Seven Deadly Sins of **PRIDE, GREED, LUST, ANGER, GLUTTONY, ENVY** and **SLOTH.**
>
> "All these failings generate **FEAR**, a soul-sickness in its own right."
> (*Twelve Steps and Twelve Traditions*, pp. 48, 49)

Adding **FEAR** to the Seven Deadly Sins results in a checklist with eight liabilities. When we compare these liabilities to the ones used in the Back to Basics Beginners' Meetings, we find the lists, for all practical purposes, are identical.

Twelve and Twelve List of Liabilities	*Back to Basics* List of Liabilities
Pride - - - - - - - - - - - - - - - - - - -	False Pride
Greed - - - - - - - - - - - - - - - - - - -	-Dishonesty
Lust - - - - - - - - - - - - - - - - - - -	-Jealousy
Anger - - - - - - - - - - - - - - - - - -	-Resentment
Gluttony - - - - - - - - - - - - - - - -	-Selfishness
Envy - - - - - - - - - - - - - - - - - -	Envy
Sloth - - - - - - - - - - - - - - - - - -	Laziness
Fear - - - - - - - - - - - - - - - - - - -	-Fear

Whether we use four, six, eight or seventeen assets and liabilities, the process is the same. The checklist is a very efficient tool for identifying and removing the shortcomings that have blocked us from the God of our understanding and the spiritual solution to our alcoholism.

When Dr. Bob died on November 16, 1950, Alcoholics Anonymous was still in its infancy, as was the technology for preserving the spoken word. Because of this, very little of what Dr. Bob had to say about our miraculous program was ever recorded.

He may have been a man of few words, but what Dr. Bob communicated in the September 1948 issue of *The A.A. Grapevine* clearly demonstrates his devotion and commitment to A.A.'s "original," God-based **"design for living."** In one paragraph, he describes the sheer simplicity of the Twelve Steps and states that, when they are taken "under divine guidance," they provide a practical solution for all of our problems:

> "As finally expressed and offered, they [the Twelve Steps] are simple in language, plain in meaning. They are workable by any person having a sincere desire to obtain and keep sobriety. The results are the proof. Their simplicity and workability are such that no special interpretations, and certainly no reservations, have ever been necessary. And it has become increasingly clear that the degree of harmonious living which we achieve is in direct ratio to our earnest attempt to follow them under divine guidance to the best of our ability." [39]

The Beginners' Meetings are a very effective and highly successful way to take the Twelve Steps and carry A.A.'s lifesaving message of recovery to others. As Dr. Bob so simply and profoundly put it, **"The results ARE the proof."**

"It works—it really does."

---

39 Anonymous, ***Dr. Bob and the Good Oldtimers*** (New York, NY: Alcoholics Anonymous World Services, Inc., 1980) 227

Appendices

Appendices

Handouts for the Alcoholics Anonymous Beginners' Meetings

Summary of Handouts for the Four One-Hour Sessions

Minneapolis Record Indicates that 75% are Successful in A.A.

Suggested Guidelines for Beginners' Meetings: "For the Newcomer" and "For the Sponsor or Sharing Partner"

The Directions for Taking the Twelve Steps

Fourth Step Inventory (Blank)

Fourth Step Inventory (Example)

Explanation of Terms: Fourth Step Assets and Liabilities Checklist

Test for Self-will vs. God's Will

How to Listen to God Pamphlet

The Twelve Steps of Alcoholics Anonymous

The Alcoholics Anonymous Beginners' Meetings

Handouts for the Four One-Hour Sessions

Session # 1: Overview and Step One

Session # 2: Steps Two, Three and Four

Session # 3: Steps Five, Six, Seven, Eight and Nine

Session # 4: Steps Ten, Eleven and Twelve

(No Handouts)

Note: Many Meeting Leaders distribute the handouts as a twelve-page stapled packet along with separate Moral Inventory sheets for Session # 2.

MINNEAPOLIS RECORD INDICATES THAT 75 % ARE SUCCESSFUL IN A.A.

The Minneapolis Group, in March, 1943, inaugurated a system for keeping a record of the sobriety of members from three months on up. As a result, the following exact percentages have been arrived at:

For the Year 1945

5-yr. members	100 % successful	0 % slipped
4-yr. "	100 % "	0 % "
3-yr. "	100 % "	0 % "
2-yr. "	89 % "	11 % "
18-mo. "	90 % "	10 % "
1-yr. "	80 % "	20 % "
9-mo. "	82 % "	18 % "
6-mo. "	70 % "	30 % "
3-mo. "	48 % "	52 % "

(Of those who slipped in 1945, only 16½ % have worked back to any degree of sobriety.)

Over-all Percentages

1943	78 % successful	22 % slipped
1944	83 % "	17 % "
1945	77 % "	23 % "

Suggested Guidelines for Beginners' Meetings

For the Newcomer:

1. Your primary obligation is to attend all four sessions. If you need assistance with transportation, your sponsor or sharing partner will help you make the necessary arrangements.

2. We will read the appropriate parts of the "Big Book" to you, specifically those passages that relate to taking the Twelve Steps.

   If you have brought a "Big Book" and are able to follow along, please do so. We will announce each passage by page number and paragraph before we read it.

   If you don't have a book, we ask that you participate by listening. We will guide you through all Twelve Steps as written by the "Big Book" authors. Please follow their directions, as we read them to you, and you too will recover from alcoholism.

3. Although a written inventory is part of the process, this doesn't mean you have to do the writing. The person who is sponsoring you through these sessions can help you write your inventory, or he or she can write it for you.

For the Sponsor or Sharing Partner:

1. Your time commitment to the newcomer is approximately four weeks. After that, both you and the newcomer will be expected to assist others through the Twelve Steps.

2. During the next month, call or visit the newcomer frequently to offer encouragement and moral support.

3. Attend the weekly Beginners' Meetings with the newcomer.

4. Offer to help the newcomer with his or her inventory. If necessary, fill out the checklist based on what the newcomer tells you. Keep in mind, the newcomer may not be able to complete the inventory without your help.

5. Share your guidance with the newcomer so he or she can see how two-way prayer is working in your life.

6. Based on your personal experience, answer any questions the newcomer may have about the A.A. program or the A.A. way of life.

The Directions for Taking the Twelve Steps

Step 1 *We admitted we were powerless over alcohol—that our lives had become unmanageable.*
This Step is described on Roman numeral pages 25–32 (xxv–xxxii) and on pages 1–43.
[The directions for taking Step One are on page 30, paragraph 2, lines 1-3.]

Step 2 *Came to believe that a Power greater than ourselves could restore us to sanity.*
This Step is described on pages 44–60.
[The directions for taking Step Two are on page 47, paragraph 2, lines 1-3.]

Step 3 *Made a decision to turn our will and our lives over to the care of God <u>as we understood Him</u>.*
This Step is described on pages 60–63.
[The directions for taking Step Three are on page 63, paragraph 2, lines 1-8.]

Step 4 *Made a searching and fearless moral inventory of ourselves.*
This Step is described on pages 63–71.
[The directions for taking Step Four are on page 64, paragraph 1, lines 1-9; paragraph 2, lines 1-6 (*Assets and Liabilities Checklist*); page 64, paragraph 3, lines 1-2, 6-9 (*Resentments*); page 68, paragraph 1, lines 1-3 (*Fears*); and page 69, paragraph 1, lines 1-6 (*Harms*).]

Step 5 *Admitted to God, to ourselves, and to another human being the exact nature of our wrongs.*
This Step is described on pages 72–75.
[The directions for taking Step Five are on page 75, paragraph 1, lines 1-4; paragraph 2, lines 1-2.]

Step 6 *Were entirely ready to have God remove all these defects of character.*
This Step is described on pages 75–76.
[The directions for taking Step Six are on page 76, paragraph 1, lines 3-5.]

Step 7 *Humbly asked Him to remove our shortcomings.*
This Step is described on page 76.
[The directions for taking Step Seven are on page 76, paragraph 2, lines 1-7.]

The Directions for Taking the Twelve Steps
(Continued)

Step 8   *Made a list of all persons we had harmed, and became willing to make amends to them all.*
This Step is described on page 76.
[The directions for taking Step Eight are on page 76, paragraph 3, lines 2-5.]

Step 9   *Made direct amends to such people wherever possible, except when to do so would injure them or others.*
This Step is described on pages 76–84.
[The directions for taking Step Nine are on page 76, paragraph 3, lines 6-11.]

Step 10   *Continued to take personal inventory and when we were wrong promptly admitted it.*
This Step is described on pages 84–85.
[The directions for taking Step Ten are on page 84, paragraph 2, lines 1-14.]

Step 11   *Sought through prayer and meditation to improve our conscious contact with God <u>as we understood Him</u>, praying only for knowledge of His will for us and the power to carry that out.*
This Step is described on pages 85–88.
[The directions for taking Step Eleven are on page 86, paragraph 1, lines 1-14 (*When We Retire*); paragraph 2, lines 1-5 (*Upon Awakening*); page 87, paragraph 3, lines 1-3, page 88, lines 1-7 (*Throughout The Day*).]

Step 12   *Having had a spiritual awakening as the result of these steps, we tried to carry this message to alcoholics, and to practice these principles in all our affairs.*
This Step is described on pages 89–103 and pages 567–568.
[The directions for taking Step Twelve are on page 89, paragraph 1, lines 4-5.]
(*Instructions on how to carry A.A.'s lifesaving message of recovery to others can be found throughout pages 89–103.*)

Fourth Step Inventory

Assets and Liabilities Checklist from the "Big Book"

pg. 64:1(1-7); pg. 64:3(1-9); pg. 68:1(1-3); pg. 69:1(1-6:edited)

Liabilities Watch for—		Assets Strive for—
Resentment		Forgiveness
Fear		Faith
Selfishness		Unselfishness
Dishonesty		Honesty
False Pride		Humility
Jealousy		Trust
Envy		Contentment
Laziness		Action

Assets and Liabilities Checklist

Fourth Step Inventory

Assets and Liabilities Checklist from the "Big Book"
pg. 64:1(1-7); pg. 64:3(1-9); pg. 68:1(1-3); pg. 69:1(1-6:edited)

Liabilities Watch for—					Assets Strive for—
Resentment	Ex	Myself	Court	God	Forgiveness
Fear	Court	Relapse	Health		Faith
Selfishness	Ex	Employer	Friend #1		Unselfishness
Dishonesty	Ex	Myself	Employer	Friend #2	Honesty
False Pride	God	Employer			Humility
Jealousy	Family Member				Trust
Envy					Contentment
Laziness	Ex	Employer	Myself		Action
Shame	Friend #2				Self-respect

Example of Assets and Liabilities Checklist with Eight Step Amends List

Explanation of Terms
Fourth Step Assets and Liabilities Checklist

In the late 1930's, Dr. Bob, one of the cofounders of Alcoholics Anonymous, developed an Assets and Liabilities Checklist, which he used to take thousands of newcomers through the inventory and restitution process. Since then, various checklists have been used by sponsors, spiritual advisors, and sharing partners to bring those **"interested in a spiritual way of life"** to a greater understanding of the shortcomings that have prevented them from finding a spiritual solution to their difficulties, a solution that is based upon establishing an intimate, two-way relationship with the **"One who has all power."**

We have defined these shortcomings–the liabilities that have been blocking us from this **"Power"**–in a way that, hopefully, will provide a clearer understanding of their meaning:

RESENTMENT is the consequence of being angry or bitter toward someone for an extended period of time over some real or imagined insult. It is a hostile or indignant attitude in response to an alleged affront or personal injury.

FEAR is being afraid of losing something we have or not getting something we want. It manifests itself in many ways including phobia, terror, panic, anxiety and worry.

SELFISHNESS is concern only for ourselves, our own welfare or pleasure, without regard for, or at the expense of, others.

DISHONESTY involves theft or deception. It includes taking things that don't belong to us, cheating people out of what is rightfully theirs, and lying to or withholding the truth from others.

FALSE PRIDE is either feeling better than or less than someone else. Feelings of superiority include prejudice about race, education or religious beliefs, and sarcasm–putting someone else down to make us feel better about ourselves. Feelings of inferiority include self-pity, which is excessive concern about our own troubles, and low self-esteem–the lack of self-worth or self-respect.

JEALOUSY has to do with people–being suspicious of another's motives or doubting the faithfulness of a friend.

ENVY has to do with things–wanting someone else's possessions.

LAZINESS means lacking the will or the desire to work. Procrastination, which is postponing or delaying an assigned job or task, is a form of laziness.

Test for Self-will vs. God's Will
From the "Big Book" of Alcoholics Anonymous

Self-will	God's Will

Fourth Step Test

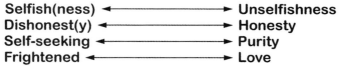

Selfish(ness) ←——————→ Unselfishness
Dishonest(y) ←——————→ Honesty
Self-seeking ←——————→ Purity
Frightened ←——————→ Love

"Where had we been selfish, dishonest, self-seeking and frightened?"
(*A.A.*, p. 67, para. 2, lines 3-4)

Tenth Step Test

Selfishness ←——————→ Unselfishness
Dishonesty ←——————→ Honesty
Resentment ←——————→ Purity
Fear ←——————→ Love

"Continue to watch for selfishness, dishonesty, resentment, and fear."
(*A.A.*, p. 84, para. 2, lines 8-9)

Eleventh Step Test

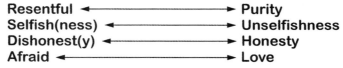

Resentful ←——————→ Purity
Selfish(ness) ←——————→ Unselfishness
Dishonest(y) ←——————→ Honesty
Afraid ←——————→ Love

"Were we resentful, selfish, dishonest or afraid?"
(*A.A.*, p. 86, para. 1, lines 2-3)

HOW TO LISTEN TO GOD

These are a few simple suggestions for people who are willing to make an experiment. You can discover for yourself the most important and practical thing any human being can ever learn--how to be in touch with God.

All that is needed is the *willingness to try it honestly*. Every person who has done this consistently and sincerely has found that it really works.

Before you begin, look over these fundamental points. They are true and are based on the experience of thousands of people.

1. God is alive. He always has been and He always will be.

2. God knows everything.

3. God can do anything.

4. God can be everywhere--all at the same time. (These are the important differences between God and us human beings).

5. God is invisible--we can't see Him or touch Him--but, *God is here*. He is with you now. He is beside you. He surrounds you. He fills the room or the whole place where you are right now. He is in you now. He is in your heart.

6. God cares very much for *you*. He is interested in you. He has a plan for your life. He has an answer for every need and problem you face.

7. God will tell you all that you *need* to know. He will not always tell you all that you *want* to know.

8. God will help you do anything that He asks you to do.

9. Anyone can be in touch with God, anywhere and at any time, *if the conditions are obeyed.*

These are the conditions:

- To be quiet and still
- To listen
- To be honest about every thought that comes
- To test the thoughts to be sure that they come from God
- To obey

- A wrong relationship in my life I will not give up;
- A restitution I will not make;
- Something God has already told me to do that I will not obey.

Check these points and be honest. Then try listening again.

10. *Mistakes*

Suppose I make a mistake and do something in the name of God that isn't right? Of course we make mistakes. We are human with many faults. However, *God will always honor our sincerity.*

He will work around and through every honest mistake we make. He will help us make it right. *But, remember this!* Sometimes when we do obey God, someone else may not like it or agree with it. So when there is opposition, it doesn't always mean you have made a mistake. It can mean that the other person doesn't want to know or to do what is right.

Suppose I fail to do something that I have been told and the opportunity to do it passes? There is only one thing to do. Put it right with God. Tell Him you're sorry. Ask Him to forgive you, then accept His forgiveness and begin again. God is our Father--He is not an impersonal calculator. He understands us far better than we do.

11. *Results*

We never know what swimming is like until we get down into the water and try. We will never know what this is like until we sincerely try it.

Every person who has tried this honestly finds that a wisdom, not their own, comes into their minds and that a Power greater than human power begins to operate in their lives. It is an endless adventure.

There is a way of life, for everyone, everywhere. Anyone can be in touch with the living God, anywhere, anytime, *if we fulfill His conditions:*

When man listens, God speaks.
When man obeys, God acts.

This is the law of prayer.

God's plan for this world goes forward through the lives of ordinary people who are willing to be governed by Him.

Written in the late 1930's by John E. Batterson
(A personal friend of Dr. Bob's--co-founder of A.A.)

Distributed by: Wally P., Archivist / Historian / Author
P.O. Box 91648, Tucson, AZ 85752-1648 - Tel: (520) 297-9348 / Fax: (520) 297-7230

So, with these basic elements as a background, here are specific suggestions on *How to Listen to God:*

1.   Take Time

Find some place and time where you can be alone, quiet and undisturbed. Most people have found that the early morning is the best time. Have with you some paper and pen or pencil.

2.   Relax

Sit in a comfortable position. Consciously relax all your muscles. Be loose. There is no hurry. There needs to be no strain during these minutes. God cannot get through to us if we are tense and anxious about later responsibilities.

3.   Tune In

Open your heart to God. Either silently or aloud, just say to God in a natural way that you would like to find His plan for your life--you want His answer to the problem or situation that you are facing just now. Be definite and specific in your request.

4.   Listen

Just be still, quiet, relaxed and open. Let your mind go "loose." Let God do the talking. Thoughts, ideas, and impressions will begin to come into your mind and heart. Be alert and aware and open to every one.

5.   Write!

Here is the important key to the whole process. Write down everything that comes into your mind. *Everything.* Writing is simply a means of recording so that you can remember later. *Don't* sort out or edit your thoughts at this point.

Don't say to yourself:
        This thought isn't important;
        This is just an ordinary thought;
        This can't be guidance;
        This isn't nice;
        This can't be from God;
        This is just me thinking…. etc.

Write down everything that passes through your mind:
        Names of people;
        Things to do;
        Things to say;
        Things that are wrong and need to be made right.

Write down everything:
        Good thoughts - bad thoughts;

        Comfortable thoughts - uncomfortable thoughts;
        "Holy" thoughts - "unholy" thoughts;
        Sensible thoughts - "crazy" thoughts.

Be honest! Write down *everything!* A thought comes quickly, and it escapes even more quickly unless it is captured and put down.

6.   Test

When the flow of thoughts slows down, stop. Take a good look at what you have written. *Not every thought we have comes from God.* So we need to test our thoughts. Here is where the written record helps us to be able to look at them.

   a.   Are these thoughts completely *honest, pure, unselfish and loving?*

   b.   Are these thoughts in line with our duties to our family--to our community?

   c.   Are these thoughts in line with our understanding of the teachings found in our spiritual literature?

7.   Check

When in doubt and when it is important, what does another person who is living two-way prayer think about this thought or action? More light comes in through two windows than one. Someone else who also wants God's plan for our lives may help us to see more clearly.

Talk over together what you have written. Many people do this. They tell each other what guidance has come. This is the secret of unity. There are always three sides to every question--your side, my side, and the right side. Guidance shows us which is the right side--not who is right, but what is right.

8.   Obey

Carry out the thoughts that have come. You will only be sure of guidance as you go through with it. A rudder will not guide a boat until the boat is moving. As you obey, very often the results will convince you that you are on the right track.

9.   Blocks

What if I don't seem to get any definite thoughts? God's guidance is as freely available as the air we breathe. If I am not receiving thoughts when I listen, the fault is not God's.

Usually it is because there is something *I will not do:*
   - Something wrong in my life that I will not face and make right;
   - A habit or indulgence I will not give up;
   - A person I will not forgive;

THE TWELVE STEPS OF ALCOHOLICS ANONYMOUS

1. We admitted we were powerless over alcohol–that our lives had become unmanageable.
2. Came to believe that a Power greater than ourselves could restore us to sanity.
3. Made a decision to turn our will and our lives over to the care of God *as we understood Him*.
4. Made a searching and fearless moral inventory of ourselves.
5. Admitted to God, to ourselves, and to another human being the exact nature of our wrongs.
6. Were entirely ready to have God remove all these defects of character.
7. Humbly asked Him to remove our shortcomings.
8. Made a list of all persons we had harmed, and became willing to make amends to them all.
9. Made direct amends to such people wherever possible, except when to do so would injure them or others.
10. Continued to take personal inventory and when we were wrong promptly admitted it.
11. Sought through prayer and meditation to improve our conscious contact with God *as we understood Him*, praying only for knowledge of His will for us and the power to carry that out.
12. Having had a spiritual awakening as the result of these steps, we tried to carry this message to alcoholics, and to practice these principles in all our affairs.